THE TEN-YEAR TURNAROUND

Transform Your Personal Finances and
Achieve Financial Freedom in the Next Ten Years

D1473873

"Massive financial success requires massive action. *The Ten-Year Turnaround* provides the information and motivation you need to IGNITE toward true financial freedom."

John Lee Dumas
Founder,
Entrepreneur On Fire (eofire.com)

"Prospering financially is more about mindset than mathematics. *The Ten-Year Turnaround* is a guide for moving from a scarcity mindset to an abundance mindset, from a fixed identity to a dynamic identity. This book will show you how those shifts will do more to release wealth than degrees, promotions, inheritance, luck or the lottery."

Dan Miller
New York Times bestselling author of
48 Days to the Work You Love (48days.com)

"If you're tired of being broke or just haven't attained the financial success you're looking for, *The Ten-Year Turnaround* is the book for you. While there are many good personal finance books that teach you how to manage your money better, *The Ten-Year Turnaround* actually teaches you how to create more economic value, increase your income over time and invest your money wisely for lifetime wealth."

Jaime Masters
Founder,
Eventual Millionaire (eventualmillionaire.com)

"I found Matt's plan for achieving financial goals in *The Ten-Year Turnaround* extremely refreshing. While many authors would try to tell you that the time it takes to achieve financial success can be measured in minutes or a few hours a week, Matt tells you the way it is with a very concrete plan that is both realistic and achievable in terms of time and effort. So, while 10 years might seem like a long time, I think just about anyone would be extremely satisfied if they accomplished half of what Matt has been able to accomplish during that time. *The Ten-Year Turnaround* will give you the knowledge and plan that you need to achieve your financial goals."

Spencer Haws
Founder,
Niche Pursuits (nichepursuits.com)

THE TEN-YEAR TURNAROUND

Transform Your Personal Finances and
Achieve Financial Freedom in the Next Ten Years

MATTHEW PAULSON

Published by American Consumer News, LLC.
First edition: May 2016
ISBN: 978-0-9905300-2-2

Cover design: Ellen Jesperson (ellenize.com)
Editing: Craft Your Content (craftyourcontent.com)
Proofreading: Rebecca McKeever (siouxfallsgraphicdesign.com)
Book Design: James Woosley (jameswoosley.com)
Printing: Amazon CreateSpace

Dedication

To my children, Micah and Adylin, I love you more than anything in the world. You provide all of the hope, inspiration, and joy that I need to get up early every day and continue to grow my businesses.

To my wife Karine, thank you for continuing to support and encourage me in everything I do. Thank you for not shaking your head at me whenever I come up with a crazy new business idea, and thank you for allowing me the opportunity to provide for our family in unique and creative ways. Most importantly, thank you for being my best friend.

Table of Contents

Introduction:
My Ten-Year Turnaround

It was August of 2004. I would be starting my first year of college in a few short weeks. My new school, Dakota State University, was located in Madison, South Dakota, which boasts a population of just 7,000 people. Madison has only a single grocery store and a handful of restaurants and retail stores to choose from. I was excited to start my computer science degree, but had no idea how I was going to pay for it. I was flat broke and had less than $500 in my checking account. I had to come up with $5,000 out of pocket each year to pay the tuition and fees that weren't covered by the few small scholarships I received and the federal student loan I had taken out. My parents couldn't afford to help me pay for college. If I was going to be able to afford to come back to school during the spring semester, I desperately needed a part-time job during the school year.

I got in my 1995 Dodge Intrepid on a hot summer day and drove to the small college town where I would be going to school, hoping to find a part-time job. Since I had worked at a gas station in high school, I applied for jobs at both of the service stations in town. I looked into finding work on campus, but quickly found out that freshmen only get hired on campus if they qualify for Federal Work Study—due to my parents' income, I didn't. I applied to work at Madison's lone grocery store and the two small department stores in town. I put in applications at a few retailers on Egan Avenue (Madison's main street) and even applied to McDonald's as a last resort, in case I couldn't find anything else.

As you might have predicted, the only place that actually called me back was McDonald's. I had absolutely no money to my name and no other way to make any. Working at McDonald's as a fry cook for $6.50 an hour was the only way that I could make tuition for the spring semester.

There was a lot not to like about working at McDonald's. Management would regularly schedule me to work from 4 PM until midnight when I had classes at 8 AM the next morning. I would spend hours on end in a hot kitchen standing at a deep fryer, cooking French fries and fried chicken at 350 degrees. It was also my job to wash grease-soaked dishes for hours at a time. There were a few fun people to work with, but there was also an uptight manager who made it his personal mission to ensure that I hated my job. I almost always came home covered in grease and dirty dish water. Even after taking a shower, I would still smell like french fries. The one small benefit was that McDonald's allowed employees to buy food at half-price before and after their shifts. I'm pretty sure I lived almost entirely on the Dollar Menu™ during my freshman year.

During that year, I allowed myself $100 per month to live off. The rest of the money I earned had to go to pay my tuition bill. I couldn't afford to go out to eat with my friends. I couldn't afford to go to the movies. I couldn't afford to take a weekend trip to anywhere that anyone would actually want to go to. Most of the $100 went to put gas in my car and buy a few meager groceries. Thankfully, my parents covered my health insurance and car insurance while I was in school, and I'm incredibly grateful for the help they provided. While I had the basic necessities of life taken care of, there wasn't anything left over at the end of the month.

Enough is Enough

A couple of months into my spring semester, I decided that I had had enough. I was sick and tired of coming home from McDonald's at midnight covered in dish water and congealed grease. I was done being ordered around by a tyrant manager who enjoyed assigning me the most menial and disgusting work available. I was fed up with being broke and unable to scrape together a few dollars for movies or any other forms of entertainment. I didn't know what I was going to do the next school year, but it sure wasn't going to be slaving over a deep fryer or a kitchen sink. I was going to turn my life around entirely, and it was going to start with my job.

As I've noted, the best work opportunities for Dakota State University students were on-campus jobs. I made a list of every on-campus job that wasn't funded by Work Study and applied to most of them. The only two departments I skipped over were food service and facilities maintenance, because I didn't want a repeat of my experience at McDonald's. I also joined a number of university clubs so that I looked well-rounded to the faculty members who would be evaluating applications. I slaved over the applications and made sure to get them in early so that I would have a good chance of being considered. While most of the jobs I applied for on campus said no, three of them said yes. My hard work had paid off. I really wanted to pay off my student loans and have some money to spend freely, so I decided to take on all three positions.

In the fall, the College of Business and Information Systems offered me my first on-campus job. It was an incredibly sweet deal that paid $15 an hour for 11 hours per week of work. I helped manage a computer lab, built a variety of websites for organizations on campus and did whatever else they told me to. The second job involved working as a study skills tutor for remedial students at the Student Success Center on campus. That job paid around $7 an hour for six hours of work per week. The third job was writing for the campus newspaper, The Trojan Times. I was the News Editor during my first two years at the paper and served as the Editor-In-Chief during my senior year. While that job didn't pay much, it was the first opportunity that I had to write professionally. Between these three positions during sophomore year and the summer job working at a gas station in my hometown, I was able to increase my income from $13,000 in my freshman year to more than $30,000 during my sophomore year.

While making $30,000 in a year isn't something that anyone is going to do a whole lot of bragging about, it did make me recognize that my financial situation wasn't carved in stone. If I was willing to work hard, improve my skill set and take advantage of opportunities when they appeared, I could dramatically change my financial lot in life. I may have been broke at that moment, but I didn't have to be broke forever. I had no idea how successful I would become during the next ten years. However, I knew that if I was willing to learn and take advantage of the right opportunities, I could create dramatically more wealth than any of my classmates.

My First Big Opportunity

During the fall semester of my junior year in college, I had a relatively low academic workload and decided to take on a side project in order to flex my writing muscles and learn more about web design. The end result was my now-defunct personal finance blog, American Consumer News. The first iteration of the blog was called Getting Green and it was hosted on a free Blogger account. I literally spent no money getting it started – because I didn't need to, but also because I didn't have a ton of extra money sitting around. American Consumer News went live on December 26th, 2006: I had officially become a personal finance blogger.

I had no idea that you could actually make meaningful amounts of money writing a personal finance blog, but very soon I started to receive emails from companies that wanted to pay me to put their ads on my website. Companies like Mint.com and Prosper.com that target savvy consumers knew that their target audience was on websites like mine, and they were happy to pay $150 per month for an ad slot on my website. At the same time, a company called Associated Content started paying people five to fifteen dollars to write articles on just about any subject. Since you didn't have to give them exclusivity on anything that you wrote, I re-submitted all my articles to them and made $500 to $1,500 per month from Associated Content for nearly a year.

During my first year of running an online business, I made a whopping $12,600 between website sponsorships, Google AdSense and Associated Content. The business didn't really take off until 2008, when I had the idea to run multiple personal finance blogs at once. I figured that if advertisers were willing to buy ads on one of my websites, they might be willing to buy multiple ads on multiple websites. I knew I couldn't do all of the writing myself, so I hired a handful of writers and had them write for my websites for six to eight dollars an article. At one time, we had five different personal finance blogs running and a team of seven writers cranking out articles. During that business' peak in 2008 and 2009, I stopped writing altogether and was taking home around $60,000 each year after expenses.

My time at Dakota State University came to an end in May 2009, when I completed the two degrees I had been working toward. During my graduation ceremony, then South Dakota Governor Mike Rounds gave the commencement speech. He spoke about how universities can create opportunities for students to do great things, and highlighted me and my business as an example of what was possible for students to achieve. I was the only student mentioned by name during his speech. The governor's words confirmed to me that my financial turnaround was getting some real traction and others were starting to notice.

After college, I moved to Sioux Falls, South Dakota to be closer to my then girlfriend (now wife) and work at a local website design agency as a programmer. While my day job paid around $50,000 per year, I didn't have the guts to try to go full time with my business, because I didn't think the business model was sustainable over the long term. The business slowly began to unravel in 2010. The social media marketing strategies we used to attract traffic over the years became less effective, and Google began to punish websites like mine that sold link advertisements.

The final nail in the coffin for American Consumer News happened on February 23rd, 2011, when Google updated its search algorithm to penalize websites that had a lot of short-form content, which they viewed as non-authoritative. Just about every personal finance blog got hammered by this change (known as the Panda Update), and my websites were no exception. More than 50% of my website traffic disappeared overnight and revenue immediately started dropping. The business became a shadow of its former self, making just a few thousand dollars each month. Eventually, I cut my losses on my personal finance blogs and sold them off.

The MarketBeat Story

I had been knocked to the ground by being too reliant on a single marketing strategy. If I wanted to make a go of running a real online business, I knew that I would need to do something different. I would need to develop a business that leveraged multiple marketing channels at once and still generated revenue even when a given marketing channel dried up.

The one website that survived Google's algorithm update was an investing news website called American Banking and Market News (now called MarketBeat.com). It didn't rely on website search traffic, and so continued to receive a few thousand visitors per day from places like MSN Money, Twitter, MarketWatch and Yahoo Finance. There was a significant opportunity to report financial and investing news through American Banking and Market News, and reporting quickly became the core of my company.

We immediately recognized that many investing news websites promoted their products and services with a lot of hype and sizzle. Inevitably, their products and services would fail to meet the expectations raised by their marketing material, and their customers would leave dissatisfied. We set ourselves apart by only offering raw financial data, information and news, so that our subscribers could do their own analysis. Even now, we will never try to convince our subscribers to follow a specific investment strategy or buy a specific stock.

MarketBeat also gained a lot of initial traction by offering the most comprehensive summary of investment analysts' stock ratings on the web. There were a lot of places on the web that reported analysts' ratings and recommendations, but they were all incomplete. We found every data provider that offered analysts' ratings and compiled them into a single database, more comprehensive than any other source online. Reporting on analysts' ratings changes continues to be the most used feature of MarketBeat.com.

MarketBeat has published financial news on our network of websites since the business began in 2011. We also publish a summary of top news headlines and analysts' ratings changes in our daily email newsletter, MarketBeat Daily Ratings. We have been able to grow our newsletter to more than 400,000 subscribers in the last five years. We also sell a variety of premium subscriptions to our newsletter subscribers that range from $15 to $35 per month. Finally, MarketBeat offers a selection of web-based research tools on its website and a mobile app called StockAid.

The business generated $276,000 during its first full year of operations in 2011. As I grew my email list, integrated new marketing channels and discovered new ways to attract advertisers, the company's revenue skyrocketed. I quit my day job in 2012 to go full-time with my business. By 2016, the business had grown to more than $3 million while maintaining a profit margin of 82%.

Where I Am in 2016

A lot has changed in my life during the last decade. In the fall of 2004, I was a broke college student with a crappy job, an unimpressive income, student loan debt and a negative net worth. I now have a personal net worth of more than $10 million and an annual income of more than $2 million per year. I've had a truly massive financial turnaround during the last 10 years. We have a paid-for home, no debt to our names and a well-funded retirement portfolio. My wife and I could live off of our savings and investments for at least the next fifteen years without making any additional income. We have attained true financial freedom.

My family also has the privilege of traveling where and when we want without having to worry about the cost of travel. We firmly believe that creating memories and having unique experiences through travel brings much more joy and happiness than having a lot of possessions. Last year, we took our son Micah to Disney World for a week. We stayed in Animal Kingdom Lodge and had giraffes and other wildlife right outside of our window. We were able to spend a week in Las Vegas, watching a number of live shows and seeing Jay Leno perform on stage. Recently, we had the opportunity to spend a week in Los Angeles. We spent some time on the beach, saw the Space Shuttle Endeavor at the California Science Museum and participated in the taping of an episode of *The Price is Right* (one of my wife's lifelong dreams).

While traveling and freedom from worrying about how to pay the bills are both fun, the best part of having some money in the bank is the opportunity to be generous to those around us and to the nonprofit organizations that we deeply care about. It truly is better to give than to receive. It's incredibly fulfilling to know that hungry people have been fed, that women and children have been rescued from the sex trade, and that the poor in spirit have heard the Gospel, in part because of God's channeling of resources through my business to support these ministries and nonprofits. There's not a single possession that I own or experience that I've had that gives me as much joy as the opportunity to give.

There have been a number of other major changes in my life since 2004. I became a Christian in 2005, which dramatically affected my outlook on life and money. My wife Karine and I met in 2008 and were married in 2011. We have two wonderful children, Micah and Adylin. I completed a bachelor's degree in computer science in 2008, a master's degree in information systems in 2009 and a master's in Christian leadership in 2011. I also co-founded two other businesses, GoGo Photo Contest and USGolfTV. GoGo Photo Contest helps animal shelters raise money through online photo contest fundraisers and USGolfTV is a digital publishing company in the golf industry.

What is a Ten-Year Turnaround?

A ten-year turnaround begins with the recognition that your current financial plan won't lead to the long-term financial results that you desire. Maybe you have too much debt.

Maybe you aren't making enough money. It could be that you aren't saving or investing enough. Either your current financial plan isn't working, or it isn't working fast enough. Perhaps you have never even sat down and thought about what your long-term financial goals are and whether or not they are achievable. It might be that you've set lofty financial goals, but have no idea how to achieve them, or maybe you're doing okay in life and just wish you could get more financial progress. If you want to achieve your long-term financial goals and become financially free before you're too old to enjoy the benefits, you are going to need a new plan. That plan is the ten-year turnaround.

A ten-year turnaround is a decade-long sprint of hard work, education and wealth-building in order to transform your personal finances, achieve your personal goals and attain total financial freedom. You will develop new skill sets and abilities so that you can create value in the marketplace and increase your income. You will work harder than you ever have worked in your life. You will put yourself out there, create your own luck and seize opportunities as they arise. You will become a person of wisdom, discernment and integrity, so that you are capable of handling a large amount of wealth. Finally, you will learn essential money management and investment strategies to help you move up the wealth ladder in the most effective way possible.

As you develop new skills, increase your income and learn to manage your money better, you will create the economic engine needed to power your personal and financial dreams. The ten-year turnaround is a recognition that the best way to attain total financial freedom is to work hard over a long period of time and continue learning along the way.

At the end of your ten-year journey of personal development and wealth building, your personal finances will look fundamentally different to how they do today. Of course, there's nothing magical about a ten-year period of focus compared to a nine or eleven-year period of focus. However, I truly believe that anyone can achieve total financial freedom over a period of about ten years by following the recommendations outlined in this book. By developing a plan, increasing your income, practicing discernment and investing wisely, you can build a significant amount of wealth in much less time than you might think.

A Note About Matters of Faith

Throughout this book I make periodic references to my personal faith in Jesus Christ and how this has affected my view of money. This book isn't overtly preachy or intended to evangelize, but I think it's important to let my readers know where I'm coming from. I personally believe that everything is owned by God and that we are simply managers of his wealth (Psalm 24:1; Deuteronomy 8:17-18). I believe that giving to those in need is a fundamental part of life that cannot be ignored (Luke 6:38; 2 Corinthians 6:8-10). I also believe in the biblical principles surrounding money, such as planning for the future (Luke 14:28), that saving money is important (Proverbs 21:20), that debt should be avoided (Proverbs 22:7), that greed is incredibly dangerous (Luke 12:15; 1 Timothy 6:10), and that contentment, not wealth, is the key to personal happiness (Hebrews 13:5).

If you aren't a Christian, know that 95% of the content in this book will apply to everyone, regardless of their faith. Most of the ideas and recommendations in this book are practical wisdom that anyone can use to move toward financial freedom. If there's a paragraph that references a biblical worldview of money that you don't agree with, skip to the next paragraph. I truly believe that Christians and non-Christians alike can benefit from the recommendations in this book, and I hope that you will give this book a chance even if you have fundamentally different religious beliefs than my own.

What You'll Learn in *The Ten-Year Turnaround*

My first book, *40 Rules for Internet Business Success* (40rulesbook.com), contains a collection of principles and strategies that I've used to build my online business. My second book, *Email Marketing Demystified* (myemailmarketingbook.com), offers step-by-step guidance to any business owner wanting to implement email marketing. These two books both offer incredibly practical advice about how to succeed as an entrepreneur, but they don't show you how to become a person with the right character, mindset, knowledge and ambition to succeed in life and in business. In my third book, I've decided to take a step back and show you how you can become the type of person that you need to be in order to be massively successful with money throughout your life. Whenever I'm hanging out with other entrepreneurs, I'm frequently asked how I've had so much financial success at the relatively young age of 30. This book is an attempt to answer that question.

If you would like to become a millionaire and attain financial freedom over the course of the next ten years, this book is for you. *The Ten-Year Turnaround* blends personal finance advice and personal development experience to help you become a person with the capacity to create and maintain massive amounts of wealth throughout your life. This book is not a step-by-step financial plan that will show you exactly what financial steps to take and when to take them. Neither is it a collection of inspiring stories that provide little actionable information. Rather, this book illustrates how you can develop the mindset, the habits, and the knowledge needed to build wealth and attain financial freedom. It will also give you a better understanding of the rules, habits, and principles that I have followed to achieve significant wealth at a relatively young age. I do not claim to be a personal finance or a personal development expert. I am not a financial advisor, a lawyer, an accountant, a doctor, or any other profession that might qualify me to offer actual professional advice. As always, consult with a professional if you aren't sure about any financial move you might want to make. The ideas and strategies outlined in this book are simply what has worked for me during the last decade and I believe they will work for you as well.

The Ten-Year Turnaround is broken up into two different parts. The first half of the book focuses on how to transform your life so that you become a person capable of producing and maintaining wealth. You will learn what it actually means to be wealthy and what impact that will have on your life. We will discuss how to create a future economic vision for your life and develop a plan to achieve that vision. You will discover how to increase your income through salary negotiation and entrepreneurship. We'll explore strategies for mastering the art of personal networking, which leads to job opportunities showing up at your door. Finally, you will learn about lifelong learning and how to practice discernment, so that you can create more economic value over time and have the wisdom to make tough decisions. Some of these topics may not seem directly related to building wealth.

However, to successfully create wealth and hold onto it after you have earned it, you have to master a wide variety of complementary skills.

The second half of *The Ten-Year Turnaround* is focused on practical money management skills. While you will learn everything you need to know to become a person that can produce wealth in the first half of the book, having a great income won't do you much good unless you know how to manage it effectively. In the second half of the book, we'll examine how to create a budget that actually works for your family. You will learn about the appropriate use of credit and debt in your life and how to invest your wealth to create a lifetime income stream. We'll also explore taxes, insurance and risk mitigation. Finally, we'll cover how to effectively give to charity.

I'm not promising that you'll get rich quick by following the ideas outlined in this book. It takes a lot of work over a long period of time to achieve personal financial freedom. I first became a millionaire when I was 28 years old, which was eight full years after I had set on a path of increasing my income and becoming better with money. If you're not willing to work more than 40 hours per week or don't want to turn off the television at night, this book probably isn't for you. If you just want to get your personal finances in slightly better shape, you should probably go read a book by Dave Ramsey or Clark Howard. This book is for people who want exceptional financial success and are willing to work exceptionally hard over a long period of time to achieve it. If that's you, let's get started.

Chapter One:
Planning Your
Ten-Year Turnaround

There are very few people in the world who wouldn't like to be independently wealthy and have the ability to choose whether or not they want to work. While almost everyone would like to be wealthy, very few people take the time to consider how much money they would need to reach that goal, what they would actually need to do in order to attain that level of wealth and what implications financial freedom would have for their life.

Developing Your Dream Spending Plan

The first step toward achieving total financial freedom is setting a goal post for your journey. Identify what kind of lifestyle you want to live and determine how much it would cost to live that lifestyle. By understanding what you want your lifestyle to look like after you've achieved personal financial freedom, and knowing how much that lifestyle would cost on an ongoing basis, you can develop a long-term goal for your savings and investments. Once you hit that number, you have attained financial freedom.

It's time to start writing down your dreams. Take some time to paint a future picture of yourself. What would you do if money were no object? How many vacations per year would you take? What kind of hobbies would you have? How would you spend your time? Would you continue to work? What kind of charitable giving would you do? Imagine a future self that is fully alive, is able to do the things that you've always wanted to do and doesn't have any economic constraints holding you back from achieving your dreams. Write down where you live, what kind of work you do (if any), what kind of hobbies you have, how much you travel and what you give to. Identifying your desires for the future is the first step toward determining what kind of wealth you should target.

The next step is to start putting dollar figures next to these dreams with a dream spending plan. A dream spending plan is the budget that you would live on if money were no object. If you want to take three vacations every year like I do, you might put down that you want to have $15,000–$20,000 available for vacations every year. You might want to set aside a fixed dollar amount to give away each year or set aside a specific dollar amount to work on a hobby. Your dream spending plan will help you determine how much money you need to earn and save to achieve your dream lifestyle.

Here's a simple example of what a dream spending plan might look like:

Sample Dream Spending Plan	
Monthly Expense	**Monthly Cost**
Dream Home Mortgage Payment	$2,000
Property Taxes & Utilities	$1,000
Groceries & Eating Out	$1,000
Health Insurance	$1,500
Hobbies	$500
Travel	$1,000 (average)
Clothing	$500
Charitable Giving	$1,500
Car / Transportation	$500
Other Living Expenses	$1,000
TOTAL MONTHLY COST:	**$10,500**

Your numbers will look different from those in this example and your dream spending plan will probably change over time as your interests and desires change. Creating your dream spending plan will show you how much income you need to earn each year and will also provide the basis for your long-term savings goal. You can start living your dream spending plan as soon as you have an adequate income to support it, but eventually you will want to build up savings and investments that can cover your dream spending plan so that you don't have to work if you don't want to.

In order to cover the dream spending plan in the example above without any additional income from a job or business, you would need investments that generate $10,500 per month. If you qualify for Social Security, a pension plan or have any other passive income streams, you can deduct that amount from the amount of money that your investments need to generate each month.

We will go into detail on how to invest to create this income stream during the investing chapter of the book, but for now assume that you will need 20 times your annual desired spending in savings to ensure that you will never run out of money.

Using the example above, you would need an investment portfolio of about $2.5 million to generate the ~$125,000 per year outlined in this dream spending plan. Once you have hit the $2.5 million mark, you have attained true financial freedom because you can live your dream lifestyle without ever having to work again. Whatever the long-term savings goal you set, you should personalize it to the lifestyle that you want to live. Don't just pick an arbitrary big round number like $1,000,000 because it sounds like it will be more money than you could ever need. Set your lifetime financial goal in the context of what you want to live off of and what the money can actually do for you.

Write Down Your Dream Spending Plan Here:

Dream Spending Plan	
Monthly Expense	**Monthly Cost**
TOTAL MONTHLY COST:	

Now, take the total monthly cost of your dream spending plan, multiply it by twelve so that you know the annual cost of your lifetime spending goal and multiply that number by 20 so that you can establish your lifetime spending goal. We multiply your annual dream spending plan by 20 because we assume that you will be able to live off of 5% of your investments each year.

Total Monthly Cost x 12	
Total Annual Cost x 20	
Lifetime Savings Goal	

The Math Won't Make Sense on Day One

While $2,500,000 might seem like more money than you could possibly ever save, it's a much more attainable goal than you might think. You could reach that $2.5 million goal in 20 years by investing $3,453 per month at a 10% interest rate, or in 15 years by investing $6,225 per month. You're probably thinking, "There's no way that I could ever save that much money each month." If you never increase your income throughout the course of your life, that's probably true. If you have an ordinary income and save an ordinary amount of money, you are not going to reach the amount of wealth you desire within the next decade or two. That's not you though.

You are engaging in a ten-year turnaround. You are committing to dramatically turn around your life financially over the next decade. Part of the ten-year turnaround process is developing useful skills and abilities that others find valuable so that you can increase your income over time. If you develop a part-time business that makes as much money as your day job does, your massive savings goal becomes much more attainable. If you learn new skills or go back to school and get a much better job, your savings goal will become much more real. Unless you already have a six figure income, you will need to increase your income throughout the course of your life if you want to achieve financial freedom prior to a traditional retirement age. Don't worry though. I'm not just telling you to "go out and make more money" without actually showing you how to do it. The entire upcoming chapter is devoted to showing you how to increase your income.

Developing Your Dream Career Plan

The steps that you take to achieve your ten-year financial turnaround will look different than mine. My ten-year turnaround involved learning computer programming in a university setting, learning business on the fly and leveraging those two bases of knowledge to build internet businesses that create cash flow.

Your ten-year turnaround might involve learning sales, investing in real estate, going back to school, starting a side business or getting a better job. There are many different paths to wealth and your best opportunities will be entirely based on your ability to create value within the context of your particular strengths, abilities, skills and weaknesses. You will have to ask yourself, "What do I want to be when I grow up?" and find an answer that you both enjoy and that will allow you to create an outsized income throughout the course of your life.

This is a great time to start thinking about how you might want to create the income that will build your wealth, and to put actionable goals in place to move in that direction. Do you want to start your own business? Do you want to switch career fields to something that pays more? Do you want to become a real estate investor? Do you want to become an expert salesperson and generate large commission checks?

Just as you have developed a dream spending plan, you should also develop a dream career plan. You should write out a description of how you want to provide for yourself ten years from now and start taking the first steps in that direction. If you want a new career, start looking at schools or learning new skills that will qualify you to make a career move. If you want to start a business, start looking for your first customer. Identify what actions you can take in the next 30 days to move you toward your dream career plan.

Here are some examples of what a Dream Career Plan might look like:

- I am going to learn computer programming from courses on Udemy and Coursera, build websites for friends and family to build a portfolio and get hired at a high-end digital marketing agency. I will make $80,000 per year in my new career after three years.
- I am going to build a real-estate portfolio consisting of single and multi-family homes. Over the next ten years, I will acquire 10 properties that will generate $10,000 per month in net income.
- I am going to learn personal selling by reading 20 different sales books and selling insurance on nights and weekends. I am then going to leverage that into

a professional sales career where I earn $150,000 per year in income.

- I am going to go back to school and get a mechanical engineering degree and pursue my lifelong dream of working as an engineer. In my new job, I will earn $90,000 per year in income.
- I am going to start my own business by finding an existing business model that works somewhere else and improving upon it. If my business does well, I will make more than $250,000 per year.

Implementing your dream career plan is probably the most important part of your ten-year turnaround. If you don't become more valuable in the marketplace by improving your skill set, by switching to a new job or by starting a business, you won't have an income that's sufficient to fund your dream spending plan. While money management and investing skills are important, building an economic engine that generates a large amount of cash each year is the single best way to accelerate your journey toward financial freedom.

Of course, not every career path can create a substantial income stream. There are some careers, like teaching and military service, that offer a limited maximum income potential. If you are in a field that doesn't offer the ability to significantly grow your income over time, you may need to identify a new career path or look for ways to generate income in addition to your primary job. If you are committed to your current career path and can't significantly grow your income, look for "side hustle" opportunities as discussed in chapter two.

Write out your Dream Career Plan on the next page.

Dream Career Plan

Goal Setting

By now, you should have established your lifetime savings goal that will fund your dream spending plan, and have begun developing a dream career plan in order to achieve that lifetime savings goal.

You know what your number is to achieve financial freedom, but setting a ten-year goal without any interim goals between now and then is a recipe for disaster. You need to periodically know whether or not you're on the right track. Setting quarterly annual goals is the best way to start getting traction in transforming your personal finances.

What action steps can you take in the next 90 days to become closer to financial freedom? What can you do over the next year? By creating and hitting your quarterly and annual goals, you will begin to see the progress you are making and be more motivated to reach your lifetime financial goal.

Here are some examples of financial goals that I set during my ten-year turnaround:

- Register for and complete Financial Peace University™
- Pay off my student loan debt by the end of the next school year
- Pay off my credit cards and become debt free (except for my mortgage)
- Build an emergency fund of three to six months of living expenses
- Max-out my 401(k) plan and my Roth IRA this year
- Ask for a 10% raise at my day job by July 1st
- Attain a personal net worth of $250,000
- Give a specific dollar amount to Christian ministries and other charities this year

- Read 25 business, finance and investing books
- Reduce my mortgage debt by $50,000
- Earn $100,000 or more from my side businesses this year
- Quit my day job and go full-time with my business by December 1st
- Purchase a new vehicle with cash this spring

Some financial authors will offer a cookie-cutter, step-by-step series of goals for you to follow as you work toward financial freedom. While there's nothing inherently wrong with these plans, they don't take into account your personal situation. You may be able to create a more personalized set of goals on your own.

If you're really not sure what short-term goals you should set, consider sitting down with a fee-only financial advisor to identify the goals that are best for your situation, such as those that are affiliated with the Garret Planning Network (garrettplanningnetwork.com). Don't meet with commission-based financial advisors that receive a commission for selling you products, as these advisers have an inherent conflict of interest.

Writing Effective Goals

Not all goals are written equally well. Poorly-defined and immeasurable goals that don't have a deadline are much less likely to be accomplished than "SMART" goals. "SMART" is a commonly-used acronym for effective goal-setting that stands for Specific, Measurable, Achievable, Results-focused and Time-bound.

Here's how to write a SMART goal:

- **Specific** – Goals that are specific are much more likely to be achieved than general goals. You are more likely to complete the goal to "join a local gym and work out four days per week by June 1ˢᵗ," than you are to complete the goal of "get in better shape." Try to put as much detail into each goal as possible. Specify what action steps you are going to take to achieve that goal and what kind of results you want to see.

- **Measurable** – Your goals should have criteria to determine whether or not you accomplish your goal. If you want to increase your income this year, you might set a goal of "earn 20% more this year than I did last year by taking on a part-time job." By the end of the year, you'll know with certainty whether or not you have achieved that goal. If instead you simply set a goal of "make a lot more money than I did last year," there will be no way to tell whether or not you have accomplished it.

- **Achievable** – The goals that you set should stretch you beyond what you currently believe you are capable of doing, but not so far beyond that there's not a clear path to accomplish them. If I want to run a marathon and haven't run since high school, I should probably first set a goal of running a 5K (3.1 miles) before setting a goal to run a full marathon (26.2 miles). This doesn't mean I should never try to run a marathon, but I should set some incremental goals before trying to achieve the big goal.

- **Results-Focused** – Your goals should focus on the results you want to achieve. If you want to lose weight, you should set an objective goal of "I want to lose 20 pounds from my starting weight," in lieu of a more general, activity-focused statement such as "I am going to go on a diet."

- **Time-Bound** – Every goal should have a deadline. By giving yourself a cut-off date on a goal, you will work harder to achieve your goal by the date that you set.

Here a few examples of general goals that people might set, along with better versions of those goals that meet the "SMART" criteria:

General Goal – *I want to lose weight.*

SMART Goal – I will lose 25 pounds from my current weight by March 1st. I will do this by reducing my caloric intake to no more than 2,000 calories per day, by signing up for a gym membership and doing 60 minutes of cardio exercise four days per week.

General Goal – *I want to read more this year.*

SMART Goal – I will read 36 books by December 31st. I will accomplish this by reading for thirty minutes every night before bed. Of the 36 books I plan on reading, at least 20 of them should be non-fiction.

General Goal – *I want to pay off some debt.*

SMART Goal – I want to reduce my debt load by $15,000 this calendar year. I will do this by taking on a part-time job at Sam's Club or Costco, working 15 hours per week on nights and weekends and by re-

ducing my living expenses by at least 15%. I will focus on paying off my highest-interest credit card
first.

While this book is focused on helping you achieve your
financial goals, I highly recommend goal setting in all parts
of your life. It's very difficult to become financially successful if the rest of your life is a mess.

If you maintain your health, establish healthy relationships, have a strong spiritual life and are committed to lifelong learning, you are much more likely to be financially
successful. Here are some other areas that you can also set
goals in:

- **Fitness** – You might want to set fitness goals, such as
  losing weight or building strength. Maybe you want
  to be able to run a certain distance or bench press a
  certain amount of weight.

- **Family** – Set goals for activities that you want to do
  with your family. Maybe you schedule a weekly family game night or want to plan a family vacation.

- **Social** – As you get older, it becomes increasingly
  difficult to find time to meet up with friends and acquaintances. Consider setting a specific number of
  visits with friends for each month and list out activities that you can do with them.

- **Career** – Start taking specific steps to create more
  value for the company that you work for. Consider
  setting a goal to ask for a raise, look for a new job
  somewhere else or start a business so that you can
  increase your income over time.

- **Spiritual** – If you are religious, consider committing to spend time every morning in prayer and reading scripture, or consider committing to attend a weekly Bible study.

- **Intellectual** – Ten-year turnaround participants should always be learning. Commit to take a university class, read a certain number of books or complete an online course throughout this process.

Take some time and write out five SMART goals that you want to accomplish in the next 12 months. By writing out your goals and sharing them with friends and family, you will be much more likely to achieve them. If your goals are tangible and other people know about them, you will work harder to achieve them and thereby avoid disappointing those you told and the accompanying embarrassment.

Five SMART Goals

Write your five SMART goals in the space below. I suggest that you write out at least one financial goal, as well as four others in separate areas of your life.

1 _____
_____
_____

2 _____
_____
_____

3 _____
_____
_____

4 _____
_____
_____

5 _____
_____
_____

How Having Money Will Change Your Life

Some of the benefits of being wealthy are obvious. You generally don't have to worry about whether or not you can afford something you want. Better, you can sleep at night without worrying whether or not you're going to be able to pay your bills. The biggest benefit of having money in the bank is the freedom to live life on your own terms. Your decisions are no longer limited by what you have in your bank account. If you have enough money, you have the freedom to choose to stop working, to continue working at your current job, or move to a job that you enjoy more even if it doesn't pay nearly as well. When you have the flexibility to not work a traditional nine-to-five job, a lot of opportunities open up because you can spend more time doing things that you enjoy. I regularly spend time with my family, have lunch with friends and attend personal networking events during the workday because I have the flexibility to work where and when I want.

When you have some money in the bank, you also have the freedom to travel the world and enjoy experiences that you couldn't otherwise afford. If money were no object, who wouldn't want to spend a week at a beach resort on the coast of Maui each year? Who wouldn't want to travel through Europe and see the Eiffel Tower, the Sistine Chapel, and The Louvre? Between traveling with my wife and attending entrepreneurship conferences, I had the opportunity to get on a plane eight times last year. I was able to have some fantastic travel experiences, and I didn't have to worry about where the money would come from.

You also have the freedom to give to the people, ministries and nonprofits that you care about the most. If you have a friend, family member or acquaintance in need, you can freely help them without worrying how it might impact you. If there's a nonprofit that's doing amazing work, you have the ability to give to them. King David wrote in the book of Proverbs that "A generous person will prosper; whoever refreshes others will be refreshed" (Proverbs 11:25). This verse has rung true in my life. I receive far more joy from giving excess money to others than I do from spending it on myself and buying more stuff.

What Money Can't Do For You

While there are some real benefits to having a lot of money in the bank, being a multimillionaire won't make you dramatically happier or solve any of your personal problems. A study from Princeton University found that there's a correlation between how much money you make and how happy you are, but only until you make $75,000 per year (http://content.time.com/time/magazine/article/0,9171,20196 28,00.html). After you have the basic necessities of life taken care of, you probably won't become any happier as you amass more wealth. Don't start a ten-year turnaround plan if you think having a fat bank account is going to make you happy. You will find yourself sorely disappointed.

As you plan your ten-year turnaround, recognize that accumulating wealth will only impact areas of your life that are directly related to money. It won't automatically improve your relationships, make you a person of integrity or cause you to get in shape. You can certainly broaden your ten-year turnaround beyond your personal finances and work to improve other areas of your life, but recognize that you will have to create an independent set of goals for each area of your life that you want to turn around. While working on one's faith, relationships and health are beyond the scope of this book, many of the principles related to setting goals and creating habits to reach those goals found in this book will help you achieve success in other areas of your life as well.

I should also caution you that wealthy individuals and families face unique problems that others do not face. If it becomes public knowledge that you have a lot of money, other people will inevitably try to get some of it from you.

Would-be entrepreneurs will ask you to invest in their businesses. Nonprofits that you've never heard of will ask you for money. Financial advisors will regularly seek you out and ask if they can "help" you with your finances. In some cases, people that you thought were friends might try to guilt you into giving them money. You may also become the target of lawsuits and financial scams.

For these reasons, I recommend against ostentatious displays of wealth like luxury vehicles and million dollar homes that will give others the idea that you have more money than you need. We will discuss how to practice discernment to protect ourselves from these types of issues later in the book.

A Note for Wealthy Christians

If you are not a Christian, feel free to skip this section. If you are a Christian and happen to become wealthy, you have a biblical responsibility to be rich in good deeds, to be generous to others and to make sure that your hope is within Jesus Christ and not in your money.

The apostle Paul provides these general instructions regarding wealthy Christians in one of his letters to Timothy:

Command those who are rich in this present world not to be arrogant nor to put their hope in wealth, which is so uncertain, but to put their hope in God, who richly provides us with everything for our enjoyment. Command them to do good, to be rich in good deeds, and to be generous and willing to share. In this way they will lay up treasure for themselves as a firm foundation for the coming age, so that they may take hold of the life that is truly life. (1 Timothy 6:17-19)

As wealthy Christians, we can use our wealth to provide for ourselves and our families (1 Timothy 5:8), but wealth should never become the source of our hope or security. Rather, our hope is in Jesus Christ and his future return, which will bring restoration to all things. Jesus' parable of the rich young ruler provides a cautionary tale about what can happen to wealthy people who put their hope in money:

Someone in the crowd said to him, "Teacher, tell my brother to divide the inheritance with me." Jesus replied, "Man, who appointed me a judge or an arbiter between you?" Then he said to them, "Watch out! Be on your guard against all kinds of greed; life does not consist in an abundance of possessions." And he told them this parable: "The ground of a certain rich man yielded an abundant harvest. He thought to himself, 'What shall I do? I have no place to store my crops.' Then he said, 'This is what I'll do. I will tear down my barns and build bigger ones, and there I will store my surplus grain. And I'll say to myself, 'You have plenty of grain laid up for many years. Take life easy; eat, drink and be merry.' But God said to him, 'You fool! This very night your life will be demanded from you. Then who will get what you have prepared for yourself?'" This is how it will be with whoever stores up things for themselves but is not rich toward God. (Luke 12:13-21)

We have the responsibility to use our wealth to do the things that Jesus cared about. We are to feed the hungry, give drink to the thirsty, clothe the naked, shelter the homeless, take care of the sick and visit the imprisoned (Matthew 25:34-40). We should also use our wealth to provide for missionaries and pastors that spread the Gospel throughout the earth (Matthew 10:5-15; Philippians 4:10–20; Proverbs 3:9-10).

Finally, we are also to learn to enjoy giving, as Paul writes in his second letter to Corinth:

Remember this: Whoever sows sparingly will also reap sparingly, and whoever sows generously will also reap generously. Each of you should give what you have decided in your heart to give, not reluctantly or under compulsion, for God loves a cheerful giver. And God is able to bless you abundantly, so that in all things at all times, having all that you need, you will abound in every good work. As it is written: "They have freely scattered their gifts to the poor; their righteousness endures forever." (2 Corinthians 9:6-9)

Money Will Make You More of What You Already Are

Having a lot of money in the bank will magnify your actions. A good person with a lot of money in the bank can do a lot of good and a bad person with money in the bank can do a lot of evil.

If you are already generous at a normal income level, you will probably become incredibly generous as you begin to build serious wealth. If you are a successful business person, you will probably gain even more success when you have money, because you are less limited by capital constraints.

Don't tell yourself that you will automatically be a savvy investor, a generous person or better in business when you have more money. You need to start working on those things as you build wealth, in order to achieve those desired traits once you are wealthy.

Money can also magnify your negative personality traits. If you're an addict and come across a financial windfall, there's a good likelihood that your addiction will spiral out of control if you have the sudden ability to purchase an unlimited amount of your vice. If you are lacking in integrity, you might suddenly decide that rules no longer apply to you.

If your life contains a series of broken relationships, a lot of money will probably damage those relationships even further, as supposed friends start asking you for cash. If you have hidden parts of your life that you're not proud of, you should clean them up before you start your ten-year financial turnaround as these areas will only get worse when money is added to the situation.

Start preparing to be the person you want to be well before you build a meaningful amount of wealth. Whether you want to free yourself from an addiction, become a generous person, develop strong personal integrity, get in shape or develop better relationships, start working on those things now. It will be much more challenging to change those parts of your life ten years down the road.

Areas of Life to Clean Up

Make a list of the areas of your life that you need to clean up while you begin your ten-year turnaround:

_____

_____

_____

_____

_____

_____

_____

_____

_____

_____

_____

_____

_____

_____

_____

_____

_____

_____

Action Steps

☐ Make a list of approximately 10 things that you would do if money were no object.

☐ Develop your dream spending plan so that you can plan to pay for your dream lifestyle.

☐ Begin developing your dream career plan so that you can start increasing your income.

☐ Identify what areas of your life you need to clean up before you start building wealth.

Chapter Two:
Focus on the Income Side
of the Equation

For several years, I had the privilege of teaching Dave Ramsey's Financial Peace University™ (FPU) course at my local church. FPU teaches the fundamentals of a wide variety of financial subjects, including budgeting, debt reduction, retirement planning, saving for college, insurance and real estate. Over the years, I saw dozens of participants successfully get out of debt and get their finances into a more sustainable position. FPU does a great job of teaching participants to manage and allocate the money they already have, but the class has very little to say about how to increase your income so that you can achieve your long-term financial goals more quickly. Classes like Financial Peace University™ only focus on half of the wealth-building equation. Whatever you make minus whatever you spend is the money that you have left over to build wealth. You can increase the amount of money that you have to save and invest by reducing your expenses, but you probably won't ever have enough money to invest to achieve true financial freedom unless you significantly increase your income throughout the course of your life.

Traditional Retirement Savings Isn't Enough

Let's imagine that you make what the typical American family makes and save 15% of your income throughout your working life. In 2014, the average American family earned $51,939. If you were to save 15% of that income between age 25 and age 65 and received a 9% rate of return on your money, you would have about $3.038 million in your retirement account. That might sound like a big number, but remember that inflation will dramatically reduce your spending power in retirement. If inflation averages 3% over your working life, your $3.038 million will only be worth $839,285 in today's dollars. Most financial planners recommend that you try to live on 4% of your nest egg each year. If you were to follow this guideline, you would have created an annual income of just $33,571 in today's dollars for your retirement years. That's hardly enough for anyone to get excited about.

If you want to become truly wealthy over the course of your working lifetime, you are going to have to earn more than the typical American family income. If you wanted to become a millionaire in ten years, you would have to save approximately $5,100 per month, assuming a 9% rate of return. To save that much money each month, you would have to make $140,000 per year and live on half of your after-tax income for the entire decade. You are going to have to regularly find ways to increase your annual income so that you are capable of funding your dream spending plan. While suggesting that someone should make more money is much easier said than done, there are several different action steps that you can take to significantly increase your income in the next year or two.

Income Growth Strategy 1: Become an Expert Salary Negotiator

If you are an employee at a business or a nonprofit, your salary will depend on a variety of factors. The manager that determines your salary will pick a payroll number based on the job that you are doing, how well you are doing it, how much experience you have and what industry averages are for that position in your area. Many of the factors that determine your salary are arbitrary, which could mean that there are many other people at other companies doing very similar work to what you do, but getting paid a whole lot more. There is probably someone, somewhere, that is making significantly more money than you are and doing a nearly identical job. It's not that they're any better than you are, they just have better information or better negotiating skills than you do.

When asking for a raise or discussing your salary at a new job, you have to remember that you are entering a full-fledged negotiation. Your employer is incentivized to hire you for the lowest amount you are willing to work for in order to maximize their profit margins or free up room in their budget for other expenses. They will come to any salary negotiation with arguments and data to support that they should pay you less than you might be worth elsewhere. Come to the negotiation with just as much information to support the salary that you want to receive.

Before negotiating a salary, spend five to ten hours researching what other people in similar roles are making at other companies using tools like Glassdoor.com and Salary.com.

Come up with well-reasoned arguments why you are the best person for the job and why they should be willing to pay a premium to hire you over someone else. Be prepared to highlight your skill set and accomplishments during the negotiation. Determine in advance what salary level you are willing to accept and be prepared to negotiate benefits like additional vacations, relocation fees, the ability to attend conferences or a better than usual bonus structure.

You should also research the topic of salary negotiation by reading at least two books and dozens of articles on the subject. I recommend the book *Salary Tutor: Learn the Salary Negotiation Secrets No One Ever Taught You* by Jim Hopkinson as a good starting place for your research on salary negotiation.

While these recommendations may sound intense, effectively negotiating your salary at the beginning of your career can have an outsized impact on your lifetime earnings. According to a study that was published in the Journal of Organizational Behavior, an employee whose beginning annual salary is $55,000 rather than $50,000 will earn more than $600,000 in additional salary over the course of a 40-year career (http://eagle.gmu.edu/newsroom/843).

Having a higher starting salary will dramatically improve your lifetime earnings because any future raises will reflect your higher starting salary. There will only be a handful of times in your life when coming well-prepared to a negotiation can result in you earning hundreds of thousands of dollars over the course of your lifetime. As a future millionaire who is willing to do what it takes to reach their financial goals, you can't over-prepare for a salary negotiation.

A while back, I served on a hiring committee to help a nonprofit select a new executive director. The candidate we hired came to the salary negotiation armed with the salary range for executive directors at very similar organizations across the country. He knew what kind of benefits were common for a position like his and made well-reasoned arguments why he was worth what he was asking for. He came to the negotiation much better prepared than the board members that were tasked with negotiating his salary, and got exactly what he wanted as a result. Because he came prepared, the nonprofit ended up paying him a higher salary and giving him more benefits than the job description had originally suggested was possible.

Income Growth Strategy 2:
Ask for a Raise

Many employers won't automatically give out cost-of-living raises or pay increases simply because you've worked for them for a long time. If you never ask for a higher salary, your employer may assume that you are perfectly happy with your compensation package. Remember that your employer is economically incentivized to pay you just enough to keep you from looking for a better job opportunity somewhere else.

Unless you work for a larger company that has periodic performance and salary reviews, don't expect your employer will ever start a conversation about raising your salary. If you work hard for your employer, have become more valuable to them over time and genuinely deserve a raise, you are going to have to be the person that initiates a conversation about your salary.

The Best Time to Ask for a Raise

If you plan on asking for a raise, the timing of your request is critically important. Ask for a raise after you or the department you work for has had a big win. Maybe you went above and beyond for a customer, you made a big sale, your department completed a project on time or your projects are frequently under budget.

You are much more likely to get a "yes" when your recent success is on your employer's mind. Conversely, it's not a great idea to ask for a raise if you've recently been reprimanded or if your company's financials are in the tank.

How I Negotiated a $10,000 Raise

When I started working for a website design agency fresh out of college, I was paid around $45,000 per year for my work. I knew I could be making more than this based on the value that I created, so I asked for a raise shortly after completing a large development project that everyone considered a big win for the company. I received a 5% raise which was certainly welcome, but not competitive with what I could have been making in the corporate world.

I was a remote employee and my employer didn't have the best understanding of what someone like me should be earning in the city I lived in. I really enjoyed my job because of its flexible nature, but I probably wasn't going to get a competitive salary unless I presented something concrete to show that other companies would be willing to pay me much more for the same work.

I interviewed with a couple of other agencies and received a salary offer of $62,500 for the title of senior web developer. The offer was from an agency I wasn't all that excited about working at, but I knew I could use that offer as the basis for a significant bump in salary.

I called up my employer, told him about the offer I had received and explained to him that I really wanted to keep working for him, but the money elsewhere was too good to pass up. I asked him how close he could get me to that number in order keep me around and told him to get back to me. A couple of days later, he said he could probably afford to pay me $58,000 per year. I accepted the offer and received a $10,000 raise overnight.

How to Ask for a Raise

If you have determined that it's the right time to ask for a raise, next determine how much you would like to ask for.

Choose a number based on what you believe you are worth and what you think your employer will say yes to.

Develop a list of arguments that show the value you create for a company and how you are becoming more valuable for your employer over time.

Put your request in writing and schedule a meeting with your manager.

During the meeting, tell them that you are looking to get a raise and provide them with a summary of your reasoning.

Clarify that you don't want an answer right away, but ask them to take your written request and consider it for a few days.

Follow up with your request a few days later.

Here are some tips that will improve your chances of getting a raise:

- **Don't Ask Your Employer for a Cost of Living Adjustment** – Your employer will probably only give you a 2% or 3% raise as a cost of living adjustment raise. It will also be very easy for your manager to say, "Well, no one has given me a cost of living adjustment this year," and deny your raise.

- **Ask for Your Raise in Writing** – This will provide a clear record of your request and give something for your manager to refer back to when they are reviewing the matter.

- **Use Data to Justify Your Raise** – Every company in the world wants to create profit for its shareholder(s). If you can show how your work adds to the bottom line with tangible data, your employer will have to consider that they might lose the value you create if they say "no" to your request and you leave your job.

- **Don't Threaten to Quit** – Be as polite and kind as possible with your request. Never suggest that you're going to quit or stop working hard if you don't receive a raise. Managers would much rather reward someone they like for their hard work than bribe someone they don't like to stick around.

- **Demonstrate Increasing Value over Time** – Show your employer how you have taken on more responsibilities or have otherwise provided more value to your company since the last time you received a raise. At least theoretically, employees are paid based on the value that they create. If you create more value for your company, you can make a strong argument that you should be able to take home some of that additional value.

- **Stay Grounded in Reality** – Your employer can realistically only pay a certain dollar amount for your job without losing money. If you're asking for a salary that's higher than what they can afford to pay, your employer may decide that they don't need you anymore.

- **Don't Be Entitled** – Never ask for a raise because you've recently had a work anniversary or simply because you feel like you deserve one without anything to back that up. When you ask for a raise, it should be entirely based on data and the increasing value you bring to your company over time.

Regardless of what job you have, there is almost certainly someone somewhere in the world who is doing the exact same job that you are and is getting paid much more than you. There's no reason that you can't make the highest salary available for the type of labor that you do, you just need to work hard and negotiate for the best salary possible. If you continually add more value to the company you work for and professionally present your request for a raise, there's a good chance that you could add several thousand dollars per year to your salary for just a few hours of work.

While getting a 5% or 10% raise won't create the massive income that you're looking to create as part of your ten-year turnaround, it's a good first step toward increasing your income. Remember that your ten-year turnaround is a marathon that could consist of multiple raises, job changes or new businesses. Asking for a raise is a good early win on the path of your ten-year turnaround.

When Your Employer Can't or Won't Give You a Raise

Not every employer is in a position to hand out a raise just because you asked for one. Sometimes your employer legitimately can't afford to give you a raise and sometimes they might just think that you haven't earned one. If your employer declines your request, ask them why they are unable or unwilling to increase your salary. If they aren't able to increase your salary because they can't afford it, ask them if you could have a raise if you found a way to bring in more money for the company. If they aren't willing to give you a raise because they think you don't deserve one, ask them under what circumstances they would be willing to give you a raise. If you legitimately believe you deserve to be paid more and your employer is unwilling to give you a raise, it might be time to start looking for a job with another company.

When You Can't Make More Money Locally

If you live in an economically-depressed part of the country where there are simply no decent jobs to be found in your field, consider moving to another part of the country where jobs are plentiful and easy to come by. While moving to another part of the country might seem dramatic, it could be a great way for you to have a fresh start personally and professionally. I'm not saying this is right for everybody, but if you have nothing tying you down, aren't thrilled about where you live and are looking for new opportunities, consider moving to a more economically vibrant part of the United States.

As I write this, the unemployment rate in Sioux Falls, South Dakota, where I live, is hovering at 3.3% and new employers are moving to town regularly. Any half-decent worker looking for a job, especially in the medical, education, banking and technology fields, could move to Sioux Falls and find a job within a few weeks.

While the salaries for professional fields aren't as high in Sioux Falls as they would be in some other parts of the country, the cost of living is substantially lower than many urban centers. Look for a community that has low unemployment, strong economic growth and employers in the industries you want to work in when looking for a new place to live.

Income Growth Strategy #3: Start Your Own Business

The best way to create a massive amount of wealth throughout the course of your life is to start and grow your own business. If you were to look at the Forbes 400, a list of the wealthiest individuals in America, you would find that the list is almost entirely made up of individuals who started their own businesses or were the heirs to fortunes created by entrepreneurship.

The top ten list currently consists of Bill Gates (Microsoft), Warren Buffett (Berkshire Hathaway), Larry Ellison (Oracle), Jeff Bezos (Amazon), Charles and David Koch (Koch Industries), Mark Zuckerberg (Facebook), Michael Bloomberg (Bloomberg News), Jim Walton (Wal-Mart), and Larry Page (Google). Each one of those individuals built a wildly profitable and scalable business over the course of multiple decades.

Entrepreneurship is The Best Path to Becoming a Multimillionaire

If you want to become a multimillionaire as part of your ten-year financial turnaround, you are going to have to either start a business or buy a winning lottery ticket. With a few rare exceptions, there just aren't any jobs that are going to pay you the $250,000-$750,000 income that you need if you want to have a few million dollars in the bank by the end of your ten-year turnaround. If you want to have $5 million in the bank by the end of your ten-year turnaround, you will have to invest $350,000-$400,000 per year and earn good returns on your investment. The only way that you are going to be able to save that much money is to start and grow a successful business. Building a business isn't the only way to become wealthy during the course of your life, but it is the fastest way to build wealth.

When I incorporated American Consumer News, LLC (MarketBeat) eight years ago, the business made less than $50,000 per year and wasn't worth anything to a potential buyer. In 2016, the company is on track to do more than $3 million in total revenue, and could probably be sold to a buyer for $8-$10 million according to a few business brokers that I have spoken to.

It's taken a ton of hard work, education and perseverance to grow MarketBeat so quickly, but how amazing is it that a business worth nothing can become worth nearly $10 million over the course of eight years? I'm not suggesting that everyone who starts a business will have the same level of success that MarketBeat has had, but if you want to create a significant amount of wealth over a period of five to fifteen years, the single best way to do that is to found and grow a scalable business.

Some People Should Start Businesses, Others Shouldn't

Entrepreneurship isn't for everyone. Some people are more naturally wired to thrive in an entrepreneurial environment than others. If you are self-motivated, ambitious, willing to hustle and a bit-free spirited, you are more wired to succeed at creating your own business than someone who needs to be managed or have their hand held. Starting your own business requires a substantial amount of self-motivation and personal ambition. If you're going to succeed in business, you are going to have to turn off the television at night, say no to social engagements and work incredibly hard for years on end. If you would rather cross items off your business to-do list than catch up on the latest episode of *The Bachelor* or *The Walking Dead,* you are probably a good candidate to start a business.

Conversely, if you don't have the personal drive and ambition to make yourself work on nights and weekends, even when the chips are down, starting a business might not be the best choice for you. Starting a business requires an incredible amount of work and you will probably be disappointed in the results if you only work on it for a few hours each week.

If growing a business isn't one of your top two or three priorities in life, don't start one. Just be the best employee that you can be for another company and try to maximize your salary through the value you create for them. While starting a business is the best way to grow your income and fuel your Ten-Year Turnaround, you can still achieve significant financial success over the long-term if you can find other ways to grow your income and manage your money wisely.

What Kind of Business Should I Start?

The type of business that you should start depends on a variety of factors, including your personality, strengths, interests and goals. Here are some considerations when identifying what kind of business you want to start:

- **Don't Play David and Goliath** – Don't pick a business where you would have to upend an entire industry to be successful. Unless you have a large amount of venture capital and significant industry knowledge, it's hard to topple a well-established and profitable industry leader. We are not trying to take over the world, we are simply trying to create a healthy income stream to provide for ourselves and our families.

- **Choose a Scalable Business** – If you want to build a business that generates seven figures in revenue (or more), select a business that is not limited by the amount of time you have available or by its geographic location. Don't build a local business that can only sell to a certain area unless you plan on opening multiple locations or franchising your idea.

- **Service Businesses Beat Product Businesses** – I am personally biased toward selecting a service business over a product business because the profit margins are much better and they are generally a lot easier to start and get going. When you start a service business, you don't have to worry about manufacturing, distribution or supply chain issues. Instead, you simply develop a service, offer it to the market and start making money.

- **Innovate an Existing Business Model** – Be wary of choosing a business model that doesn't exist anywhere in the world already. If an entirely new business model was truly a good idea, somebody would probably already be doing it. Instead, find an existing business model that's already working somewhere else and find a few ways to improve upon it. While tech startups that promise to disrupt an industry might get a lot of buzz, most profitable companies are pretty boring-sounding businesses that simply offer a good product or service at a reasonable price. For every one startup like Uber that takes off, there are 1,000 failed startups that never made it off the ground.

- **Choose a Business that Matches Your Interests** – When you start a company, you should plan for it to take at least five years to build it into a profitable business. Because you're going to be working on it for so long, you really have to choose something that you can wake up excited about every day. It doesn't have to be your personal passion, but it does have to be something you are going to have fun doing and will have the energy to keep doing when you're down and out.

- **Avoid Multi-Level Marketing Programs** – Most people are now smart enough to run the other way when they hear words like "Amway" and "Herbalife," but I'm continually surprised to see how many people are still falling for the hype of multi-level marketing (MLM) programs. The reality is that most people who sign-up for MLM end up making very little or no money. I've written about this topic extensively on my blog at http://mattpaulson.com/2014/06/please-dont-pitch-me-on-your-mlm.

- **Use Your Unfair Advantages** – Everyone has something that they're better at than anyone else is. If you have unique skills, abilities or resources that no one else in your industry has, you can insulate yourself from competition and grow much faster than you would otherwise. In my case, I'm better at marketing financial content and automating tedious business tasks using software than just about anyone else. Many have tried to copy what I've done in my business, but they just can't compete because they don't have the unique skillset that I do. Identify what unique skills or other unfair advantages you have and make them the core of your business.

- **Be Mindful of Startup Costs** – One of the most common reasons that startup businesses can fail to get off the ground is because they don't have the investment capital necessary to really get their business going. For this reason, I strongly recommend that, for your first business at least, you choose a business model that requires a lot of hustle and hard work, but doesn't require a significant amount of money to get started.

It would be much easier if I could just tell you what kind of business you should start, but the reality is that not every business model is right for every entrepreneur. It would be much easier if I could just tell you to go out and start a car wash or a web design business, but it just doesn't work that way. Do your own research and find the business model that's right for you. Take an inventory of your resources, your skills and your interests, and then choose a business model based upon your personality. From this position you'll have a better vantage point for assessing your likelihood of success.

Further Reading

While the complete process of taking a business from idea to launch is beyond the scope of this book, I've written extensively about how to launch a business in my first book, *40 Rules for Internet Business Success*. You can get a copy of that book in paperback, Kindle or audiobook format on Amazon at 40rulesbook.com.

You can also learn about my favorite customer acquisition strategy, email marketing, in my second book, *Email Marketing Demystified*. You can get your copy of this book at myemailmarketingbook.com. Finally, there are a number of other books that I recommend to anyone who wants to start their own business. These are listed in the appendix of this book.

Income Growth Strategy #4: Start a "Side Hustle" Business

Going all in on a full-time business isn't right for everyone, but that doesn't mean entrepreneurship is totally off the table. You might have a high-paying or cushy full-time job that you don't want to give up, or you might have family members that depend upon the salary from your day job to keep the lights on and food on the table. Not everyone is in the position to dive headfirst into a business, and that's okay. There are still some ways that you can leverage the benefits of entrepreneurship without losing the security of your day job or putting your family at risk.

Introducing The "Side Hustle"

A side hustle is a part-time business that allows you to leverage a unique skill or ability that you might have during your off-hours to make extra money. A side hustle usually involves you selling a product or service to other individuals, such as professional photography, website design, selling art on Etsy, driving for Uber or selling an online course. Side hustles usually have incredibly flexible hours because they can't interfere with your day job by definition. While you won't make the type of money with a side hustle that you might make launching a full-fledged business, with the right side hustle, you can still make an extra $500-$1,000 per month.

I believe that anyone who isn't running a full-time business should have a side hustle of some kind or another. Side hustles are a great way to add another $10,000-$15,000 to your annual income each year. With that extra money you can pay off debt, max out your retirement and reach your long-term financial goals much faster.

Starting a side hustle will also create diversity in your income. If you ever lose your job, you'll still have some money coming in from your side hustle to get by while you look for another job.

The only people that probably shouldn't start a side hustle are those who are already full-time entrepreneurs. In such a situation, a side hustle can become too much of a distraction from your main business and cause you to lose focus.

Types of Side Hustle

There are an untold number of ways to make money on nights and weekends. I have put together a list of some potential ideas for you to consider below. You could:

- Drive for Uber or Lyft
- Work as a freelance bartender on nights and weekends
- Serve as someone's virtual assistant
- Raise chickens in your backyard
- Remove pet waste from other people's backyards
- Do voiceover acting work as a freelancer
- Play Santa Claus during the holidays
- Bake cakes for weddings and other special occasions
- Purchase a photo booth and rent it out to events
- Sell your arts and crafts on Etsy
- Referee middle school and high school sports games
- Serve as a substitute teacher for your local school district
- Offer a mobile car detailing service
- Scour garage sales for good finds and flip the merchandise on eBay
- Write on a freelance basis for an online publication
- Build websites for people and local businesses
- Clean houses
- Rent out your apartment on Airbnb
- Blog about a topic that interests you and make money with ad revenue
- Create and sell an online course

- Find a service that you can offer on Fiverr.com
- Babysit children
- Clean pools
- Fix computers
- Deliver pizzas
- Do handyman work
- Paint homes
- Work for RedBox and get paid to stock DVDs at their kiosks
- Complete jobs listed on TaskRabbit.com
- Wash exterior windows on people's homes and businesses

Use this list as a starting point to think about what kind of side hustle you might want to pursue. Don't think that you have to do any one of the thirty items listed above. Your side hustle can literally be anything legal, moral, and ethical that earns you money on nights and weekends.

Further Reading

While researching for this chapter, I came across a resource that was simply too good not to share.

Budgets are Sexy (budgetsaresexy.com) has put together a list of more than 60 different side hustles, together with experiences from people who've done them. This resource, titled "60+ Side Hustles and Counting..." can be accessed at http://budgetsaresexy.com/ways-to-make-money.

If you want even more ideas for side hustles, there are dozens of lists of different side hustles online. Just search for "types of side hustles" in Google and numerous lists will come up.

A Note About Passive Income

If you have spent more than a few minutes reading about Internet marketing, you have probably been pitched the idea of generating a passive income stream. In order to get you to sign up for a service or buy some sort of product, some marketer will try to sell you on the dream of an easy-to-set-up business that will generate income for you while you're doing just about everything but working. They will promise to teach you how to set up a passive income-generating businesses, "all for just $39.97."

The dream is that you'll have some sort of business that runs around the clock without your intervention. Hanging out on the beach? You're making money. Taking a nap? You're making money. Having dinner? You're making money. In the shower? You're making money.

Your passive income business may be a website that generates ad revenue from Google AdSense. It might be an e-commerce store with outsourced fulfillment. It could be a collection of ebooks that you sell through your website. Anything that doesn't require you to be at your computer while you're making money could be considered a passive income business.

There's only one problem with passive income businesses. They don't actually exist.

There are many entrepreneurs with businesses that generate income while they sleep, but there's nothing passive about them. The idea that you can create a business that generates significant amounts of income, that you only have to work on for a few hours per week, is a fairy tale. The mythical four-hour workweek does not exist. There's nothing passive about building businesses that generate passive income streams.

The reality is that successful business owners with "passive income" businesses work really, really hard to create businesses that generate income when they're not working. They are compulsive about finding ways to improve and grow their business. Chances are, they are working harder than you are.

How do you think they got where they are? Do you think Pat Flynn (smartpassiveincome.com) built a business that generates $100,000 per month in affiliate commissions by working four hours per week? Do you think that Tim Ferris built the "four-hour" brand by working four hours per week? Not a chance.

Yes, you can build your business in such a way that you get paid when you're not working. I'm living proof. Ten years into building my online business, I can take a day off just about whenever I want and not skip a beat.

The problem is that it will never happen if you start off only working a handful of hours per week. You'll never get anywhere because you didn't do any work up front. The occasional four-hour work week is a luxury for people who have already put thousands of hours of work into building their businesses.

If you're just starting your business, put as much ambition and effort into building and growing your business as possible. If you truly want to have a business that generates passive income, be prepared to put in thousands of hours of work to make that happen.

My Income Maximization Plan

I am going to take the following steps over the next 12 months to increase my income:

_____

_____

_____

_____

_____

_____

_____

_____

_____

_____

_____

_____

_____

_____

_____

_____

_____

Wrap-up

In order to attain complete financial freedom over the next ten years, you are going to have to increase your income so that you have the ability to save dramatically more than a typical American family. You can do this by becoming a better salary negotiator, working toward a raise, starting your own full-time business or earning extra money by doing a side-hustle.

The biggest thing that you should take away from this chapter is that your income and your career path are not static. You can earn dramatically more money over time if you start moving toward a higher income today. It is entirely possible to double, triple or even 10x your income during your ten-year turnaround, but remember that this is a ten-year process. Don't expect to double your income during the first year without dramatically increasing the economic value you create for your employer (or your customers, if you run a business). It will take a few years to learn new skills, create more economic value and find the right opportunities that will allow you to maximize your income.

Action Steps

☐ Learn about salary negotiation and be well-prepared for your next salary discussion.

☐ Ask for a raise or start looking for a higher-paying job every 12-24 months.

☐ Consider what kind of full-time business you could start in the next 1-3 years.

☐ If full-time entrepreneurship isn't for you, consider starting a side-hustle to create extra income.

Chapter Three:
How to Create Your Own Luck

There is an intangible quality that most financially success-ful people have that others don't, which I call "The Hustle Factor."

They work harder and get a lot more done than every-one else. Opportunities tend to show up on their doorstep and when the right one shows up, they immediately jump on it. They tend to be more well-known than most people in the community because they put themselves out there, inten-tionally build relationships, and regularly attend networking events. They regularly set goals and then do whatever it takes to achieve them. Quite simply, they have more hustle than everyone else.

If you want to achieve personal and financial freedom over the next ten years or so, you are going to have to hustle like you never have before. You are going to have to work harder than you ever have in your life. You will be juggling multiple projects at once and working more than the traditional nine-to-five. You are going to have to put yourself out there and make yourself known to your local business community so that the right opportunities show up at your door. By doing these things, you will find new opportunities to increase your income and accomplish substantially more than your peers who aren't undertaking the ten-year turnaround.

Taking Massive Action

If you want to make a massive financial change in your life over the next ten years, you have to take massive action. People who are extremely successful work much harder and get a lot more done than those who are merely average. They work more hours, work more efficiently, and leverage the labor of others through delegation and outsourcing. They learn more and are willing to do things that make them uncomfortable.

If you want to succeed financially, you are going to have to do more, work faster and make some mistakes. Financial success follows massive action.

You can't sort-of, kind-of have a financial turnaround by slowly implementing the recommendations in this book over the next few years. You have to get fired up and extremely motivated. Start implementing the action steps outlined in this book today. Attack your financial situation from multiple angles in order to get real traction. You'll need to increase your income, comb through your budget line-by-line, learn to invest better and become a lifelong learner—all at once. If you want to be successful in your ten-year turnaround, you are going to have to work harder, work faster, work more efficiently and accomplish more than the average person.

How to Make Opportunities Show Up at Your Door

There's a common assumption that financially successful people are luckier than others. They were born at the right time and place and had the right opportunities put before them. While this is true in some cases, more often than not successful people create their own luck by putting themselves out there, making personal connections and looking for opportunities.

If a lot of people in your community know who you are, what you are good at and what kind of work or business opportunities you are looking for, your name will be at the top of everyone's mind when an opportunity comes up that would be a good fit for you.

Over the last five years, I have built a reputation in my city as an expert in creating and growing Internet-based businesses. Because of this, the two owners of USGolfTV (usgolftv.com), a digital publishing company in the golf industry, came to me when they wanted to take their business to the next level in 2014. The wife of one of the owners regularly saw my social media postings about online business and suggested that they meet with me.

Initially, I met with them over lunch to see if I could help them out and give them some ideas. After meeting a couple of times, it was clear there was a good fit and we decided to become business partners. I acquired a stake in that company in August 2014 and was able to leverage a lot of knowledge and a little bit of time in order to grow their business.

The company more than doubled its annual revenue in the first full year we were in business together. We also grew the email list from about 5,000 subscribers to more than 75,000 subscribers. Now, I own a piece of a profitable company that I probably would never otherwise have heard of if the owners had not personally sought me out. Because of my reputation as a successful online entrepreneur, "Matthew Paulson" was the first name that came up when they started telling people they were looking for outside help to grow their online business.

Personal Networking That Works

In order to attain top-of-mind positioning for a particular industry in your community, people first have to know who you are.

Five years ago, no one in the entrepreneurial community in Sioux Falls had any idea who I was. I was a relative recluse that primarily worked at home and rarely, if ever, attended personal networking events.

As a natural introvert, I had no particular desire to make a big name for myself in my local community, until I came to the realization that I was losing out on a lot of valuable connections, potential business partners and investment opportunities as a result.

Toward the end of 2013, I decided that I was going to introduce myself to the entrepreneurial community in my city and beyond. However, I didn't want to set a fuzzy and immeasurable goal of simply being "better connected" to my community.

I decided that I would focus my personal networking efforts in three areas:

- Meeting other entrepreneurs for lunch and coffee
- Strategically attending and sponsoring local events
- Producing content to establish myself as an authority in online entrepreneurship

Making Personal Connections Through Coffee and Lunch

Like most introverts, I'm much better at having a one-on-one conversation than chatting in a large group. I figured that instead of chatting with a lot of people at once, I could simply have a lot of one-on-one conversations with other entrepreneurs. I decided that every Monday, I would ask three people if they wanted to have lunch or coffee "in the next week or two" (but mostly lunch, since I like to eat).

I started with friends and acquaintances, and then moved on to loose acquaintances and other people I had met at events. Since my first book came out, I have had an increasing number of people ask to buy me lunch, which has made the process even easier. I typically have two or three lunch dates every week with other entrepreneurs, ministry leaders and business leaders in the area.

I don't have any secret strategy to set up lunch and coffee meetings. I simply email or send a Facebook message to the person, saying that I'm interested in hearing about what's going on in their life and business and asking if they're interested in going out to lunch. Prior to having lunch with people, I'll think about a few different things that I want to ask them about so there's plenty of potential conversation topics. After I have lunch with someone, I'll put a note in my calendar 2-3 months later to see if they want to grab lunch again in the near future. That's really all there is to it.

Personal Branding Through Content Creation

The people that are most interesting to talk to at networking and community events are those who have built successful businesses. People that "someday" or "might" want to build a business (commonly known as "wantrapreneurs") just aren't all that interesting to talk to. I knew that if I was going to be able to network with successful entrepreneurs, I would have to establish myself as someone with real business chops.

I decided to start writing about entrepreneurship and began writing one article every week on my personal blog. I also actively followed people on LinkedIn, Twitter and Facebook that I wanted to meet. That way, when I ask someone if they want to grab lunch, I'm not seen as some stranger that probably wants to pitch them some multi-level marketing scheme, but as the guy whose blog posts they've been reading for the last several weeks or months.

More recently, I have begun writing books about business and entrepreneurship as a way to expand my content creation efforts and reach a wider audience. Many people that introduce themselves to me at entrepreneurship events tell me that they have read my books well before they met me.

My first two books, *40 Rules for Internet Business Success* and *Email Marketing Demystified*, serve as marketing channels that grow my personal brand and make other entrepreneurs and business people want to get to know me.

Personal Networking Through Event Attendance

I attend a number of local business, leadership and entrepreneurship conferences every year, but they aren't all good networking opportunities. Since the focus at these events is primarily on the speakers, there's just not a ton of time to talk to people.

I have had much better luck making personal connections by attending weekly and monthly meetups for people who are interested in entrepreneurship. You tend to see a lot of the same people at regular meetup groups, which makes relationship building much easier. When I attend a weekly or monthly event, my only goal is to introduce myself to one person who I haven't already met. I can usually even identify who I want to introduce myself to ahead of time by seeing who has RSVP'd to any given event on Facebook. If there's someone I don't get a chance to meet, there's always next time.

One of my favorite meetups is 1 Million Cups (1millioncups.com), which is a weekly networking event in dozens of different cities in the United States. You can usually find local business and entrepreneurship events by looking on meetup.com or by looking at events in your area on Facebook.

You should check and see if there is a co-working space in your community. Co-working spaces often serve as a community center for entrepreneurs and other business-minded people.

You could also check and see if your local chamber of commerce sponsors any local events. If you live in a city of any meaningful size, there are probably business networking events already happening. You just have to go and find them.

If there aren't any events to be found, you could be the person to start a meetup or other event, which would automatically make you the center of the new community you help create.

While the strategies that I use for personal networking might not be ideal for everyone, they have served me extremely well as a way to build a reputation as an entrepreneurial thought leader. I now have far more opportunities present themselves to me and I get asked at least once every other week if I want to go into business with someone. While most of the opportunities that show up at my doorstep aren't worth pursuing, every now and then a great business or investment opportunity will come by that's too good to pass up.

How to Evaluate Opportunities

Not all opportunities that present themselves to you will be equally interesting. If someone wants you to sign up for Amway underneath them or clean their garage for $20, you probably already know that those particular opportunities aren't worth pursuing.

While it's usually pretty easy to sniff out the really bad opportunities, some are less clear. You might not know immediately if a new job opportunity, personal networking opportunity or other business opportunity is worth pursuing, because you just aren't sure what you would be signing up for.

Here are the ten questions I ask myself when evaluating each opportunity:

- Who is the person presenting the opportunity? Are they reputable? What's in it for them?

- Does this opportunity leverage my unique skills, abilities and strengths?
- How much of my time would it take to pursue this opportunity?
- What kind of economic value would I be able to extract from this opportunity?
- Is this opportunity worth my time?
- What's the likelihood that I will be able to successfully execute on this opportunity?
- What other opportunities will I be unable to pursue if I pursue this opportunity?
- Does this opportunity fit in with my long-term goals and objectives?
- Am I genuinely excited about pursuing this opportunity?
- What additional information do I want to know about this opportunity?

Whenever you are presented with an opportunity, ask yourself the ten questions listed above to determine whether or not the opportunity is worth pursuing. If you don't have enough information to answer these questions, go out and get the information that you need and it will usually become clear if you should pursue the opportunity or not.

When you don't have sufficient information, you're bound to make mistakes. When I look back at the opportunities that I took that didn't work out, I moved too quickly on many of them and didn't have sufficient information to make an informed decision. One mistake that I have made is not independently confirming what someone is telling me. A while back, I purchased a small online business in the investment space. Everything that the seller had told me seemed to check out, but if I had taken the time to ask other people in the industry about the seller, I would have known to stay far away from the deal. It's always a good idea to ask around about anyone that is presenting an opportunity to you.

Seize Your Opportunities

People regularly ask me, "What's next for you and your business?" They think that I always have plans to pursue a big opportunity or strategy mapped out for the next several months. I never have a good answer to that question, because I jump on new opportunities right away and often have very little in terms of pending opportunities that I haven't already taken advantage of.

When an opportunity does present itself to me, I don't ask myself "When do I need to get moving on this opportunity?" Instead, I ask myself how quickly I can start taking advantage of the opportunity. When I become aware of a new potential marketing strategy for my business or learn a better way of doing something, I will usually start leveraging that opportunity within 24 hours of hearing about it.

Every now and then a big opportunity will present itself to you. This might be a shot at a new, higher-paying job, the opportunity to meet an important business leader in your community, a chance to start a new business or grow your existing business, or a gig to make a lot of extra money on the side.

When one of these opportunities shows up, jump on it right away. You don't know how long the opportunity will be available for, so don't delay. Someone else may take advantage or the person presenting it may just change their mind. Take immediate action so that you can seize the moment and be ready when the next opportunity shows up on your doorstep.

Wrap-up

If you want to achieve massive financial success throughout the course of your life, you are going to need help from mentors, business owners, and other professional networking contacts. It's very rare that someone accomplishes anything notable alone. Start building your base of personal networking contacts through one-on-one meetings, attending networking events and creating your personal brand. Begin today, so that valuable business and career opportunities can start showing up at your door.

Action Steps

- ❑ Make a list of seven things you will do in the next week to get closer to financial freedom and do one of them each day.

- ❑ In the next week, ask three people who would be valuable personal networking contacts to lunch.

- ❑ Find a schedule of local personal networking events and attend at least two of them in the next 30 days.

Chapter Four:
Learn and Discern

Many people have a very narrow view of what education looks like and what role it can play in their lives. They believe that education is simply the process of learning in a formal academic setting, a process that begins when you enter kindergarten and ends when you graduate from college. Some people even refer to graduating from college as "completing their education." After they are done with their formal schooling, they never again set out on an intentional process of learning something new and don't integrate ongoing learning into their life.

Unsurprisingly, people who are financially successful have a much broader view of education. Dr. Thomas Stanley did a study of the habits and behaviors of self-made millionaires for his best-selling book, "The Millionaire Next Door". He found that the average millionaire reads at least one nonfiction book every month. Will reading a nonfiction book every month make you a millionaire? I doubt it, but Stanley's research does illustrate the point that millionaires tend to be lifelong learners.

Self-made millionaires recognize that there is a lot about life and business that they do not know. They recognize that the world is constantly changing and that there is always new information to learn which could have a tangible impact upon their lives and businesses. They know that there are potentially game-changing pieces of information about their business or career that are currently unknown. For these reasons, many successful people have embarked on a journey of lifelong learning to become more knowledgeable and well-rounded.

If you desire financial freedom, you must expand your base of knowledge. You will need to learn about your career, about general business, about personal finance and investing, about negotiation and about a wide variety of other topics. You won't become an expert in these areas overnight, but by embarking on a lifelong journey of education you will learn about these topics and will always know more than you did yesterday.

The remainder of this chapter focuses on the power of lifelong learning.

We will explore how the power of education and hard work can help you become a better version of yourself over time. You will familiarize yourself with the practical steps necessary to continue learning throughout your life. You will also learn how to practice discernment and find answers to tough questions so that you can become a better decision maker over time.

Fixed Identity vs. Dynamic Identity

I worked at Burger King during my sophomore and junior years of high school. In terms of a part-time high school job, it could have been a lot worse. I worked with a lot of my friends and the managers were nice enough. I stopped working at Burger King during my senior year of high school when I started working at a local Amoco gas station. Five years later, I was working on my first master's degree and happened to be in my hometown, visiting my parents. I stopped at Burger King to grab some lunch and one of my old managers, Paul, was still working there – in the exact same assistant manager job that he'd been in five years ago. He asked me what I was up to these days and I told him that I was working on a graduate degree and teaching classes for Dakota State University as part of an assistantship. Paul was quite surprised by how much my life had changed and that someone was letting me teach a college class less than six years after working a cash register for Burger King. He said something along the lines of, "Really? It wasn't that long ago that you were working for us, was it?" We exchanged a few pleasantries and I went on my way.

My former manager Paul had a very fixed view of his identity. He had been a restaurant manager for years before I worked for him and would continue to be a restaurant manager for years after I stopped working for him. I'm pretty sure that he's still a manager at another local restaurant in my hometown today. People like Paul, who have a fixed identity, believe that they will always be who they are now. They generally do not have long-term goals or plan for the future. They focus on enjoyment in the here-and-now be-cause they don't believe they can have a better tomorrow. They either don't believe they can change who they are through hard work and education or they're unwilling to do the hard work necessary to better themselves. They are who they are now and nothing will change that.

Having a fixed personal identity is entirely fine if you are happy with your current job and have no aspirations to do anything more. If you have larger aspirations for life, you are going to need to adopt a more dynamic view of your identity. People with a dynamic view of their identity recog-nize that they are where they are today because of what they have done in the past, but that they can be an entirely differ-ent person depending on their hard work, learning and de-termination in the future. If you want to achieve massive personal, financial and career success, you are going to have to create a vision of your desired future personal identity and then set out to become that person.

I have always had a dynamic understanding of my iden-tity. Even when I was in high school and working at Burger King, I recognized that I could and would go off to college, get a computer science degree and find a job somewhere in a larger city as a computer programmer. Just because I was a fast-food worker then didn't mean I had to be a fast-food worker forever. In high school, my desired future identity was to be a computer programmer working at a large com-pany. In order to do that, I would need to get a computer science degree and get some practical experience doing pro-gramming work. I set out to achieve that goal and became that desired future version of myself. If you aren't satisfied with where you're at in life now and want to be more than what you currently are, begin creating a future vision of how your life might look if you accomplish all of your near-term personal, relational, career and financial dreams. After you have developed a desired future vision for your life, refer back to the guidelines on goal setting in Chapter 1. Break your vision down into tangible steps, use these to develop a plan, and set out to become that person.

How to Become a Lifelong Learner

The key to becoming a lifelong learner is to develop habits that will allow you to learn automatically over time. Learning should become a natural part of your daily rhythm, just as you brush your teeth and take a shower. Set aside 20 or 30 minutes every day to learn something new, and do it at the same time every day so that it becomes a part of your daily routine. Most people will probably read nonfiction books during their daily learning time, but you can easily substitute audiobooks or podcasts if reading does not come naturally to you. Creating a daily reading habit will ensure that you are regularly learning new things about a wide variety of subjects.

There will also be times in your life that you want to learn a new skill or dive deeply into a specific subject area. You might want to learn professional woodworking, web page design or accounting. Your daily reading habit will probably not be sufficient when you want to learn a brand new skill, especially one that you can apply in the marketplace. In this case, set aside 60 to 90 minutes of focused learning time to work on your new skill, at least four days per week. I also suggest finding a structured learning environment to help facilitate your learning. This might mean taking an online class from Coursera or Udemy, completing a workbook or auditing a class from a local college or university. Working through a structured process will make sure that you don't miss out on anything important and will push you to keep up with the material as the class or workbook progresses.

Here are a few different educational resources I have found valuable:

- **Udemy** – Udemy (udemy.com) is an online learning platform that offers more than 40,000 different courses in just about any subject matter that you can think of. The courses tend to have anywhere between four and twenty hours of video instruction and cost between $10 and $300 to take.

- **Lynda** – Lynda (lynda.com) is a membership-based online learning platform that hires experts to create online classes. Lynda is well-known for its technical courses in programs like Adobe Photoshop and Final Cut Pro, but also has a broad base of classes for software developers, graphic and web designers, photographers, entrepreneurs, animators and audio and video editors. With its $25 per month unlimited membership, Lynda tends to be more cost-effective than taking individual Udemy classes.

- **Audible** – Audible (audible.com) is the world's largest seller of audiobooks. They have a membership plan where you can download one audiobook every month for $9.95. Listening to audiobooks allows you to read while working out, in the car, or doing chores around the house. If you have a 20-minute commute to work, you could listen to an audiobook on the way to and from work every month.

- **Podcasts** – I love listening to business, personal finance, and entrepreneurship podcasts. I find that podcasts tend to offer more practical advice than business books, which often target a broader audience. You can view a list of the podcasts I listen to at http://mattpaulson.com/latestpodcasts.

- **The Kindle Store** – I read almost exclusively through the Kindle App on my iPad these days. It's far more convenient than buying books at a chain bookstore or having them shipped from Amazon. With more than 4 million books in the Kindle store, there is something for everyone. If you want to save some money, local libraries often have free ebook and audiobook rentals through OverDrive.

- **Audit University Classes** – Most universities allow non-students to audit classes for as little as $50 per credit. Auditing a class simply means you are taking a class but don't have to do any of the homework, you won't be graded and you won't receive college credit. Auditing college classes can be a great strategy if you need to learn a professional skill, such as accounting.

Should I Go to College or Go Back to School?

The traditional path of going through college after graduating from high school serves two purposes. It provides a way for young adults to live away from their parents whilst still having some guardrails to keep them out of trouble, and it theoretically prepares them for a career after college. A formal college education tends to work better when you get a degree that prepares you for professional or technical work, such as engineering, law, medicine, or technology. A college degree has far less value when you select a liberal arts degree or any degree that doesn't prepare you to do a specific job.

Given the incredible cost of a four-year college education, I would have a hard time recommending that anyone goes to college unless the degree prepares them to work in a specific industry. If you are in high school and are heading toward college, pick a degree program that will provide skills that can be easily implemented in the marketplace. You should also try to minimize your student loan burden by attending an affordable school, working part-time in college and applying for every scholarship you can think of.

If you are an adult learner and are considering going back to college, your decision to attend school should be based almost entirely on what kind of job you can get by having a college degree that you wouldn't otherwise qualify for. For example, it probably won't make sense to spend $50,000 to get a degree in social work that will earn you a job that pays $35,000 per year. If you spend $50,000 to get a computer science or engineering degree that can earn you a $90,000 per year salary, the math starts to make more sense.

While college is a good path for some adult learners, remember that what you learn is much less important than where you learn it. Employers are beginning to wise up to the reality that college degrees aren't the be-all-end-all credential that they used to be. Many employers use a college degree as a way to automatically filter out candidates, but that doesn't mean they won't hire people without college degrees. If you don't have a college degree and are looking for a way to begin a new career, I highly recommend Dan Miller's book, *48 Days to the Work You Love* (48days.com).

The book provides a strategy for working around the traditional hiring process to set yourself apart from other candidates and get noticed when you otherwise might be passed over.

College degrees are credentials that will allow you to land your first job. Don't expect that your degree will propel your entire career. After you have been working for more than a couple of years, any future employer will be much more concerned about what you are capable of doing and what you did at your most recent job than where you went to college.

When I was working at a web design agency and was considering making a switch, everyone I talked to was more interested in what kind of programming I was capable of doing and the projects I had worked on than they were in where I had gone to school. Now that I am an entrepreneur, no one ever asks me where I went to college. College can be the right move for some people, but only in the sense that it trains you to do something that other people will pay you to do.

How to Answer Hard Questions

Lifelong learning is an important component in developing new skills, increasing your income and attaining financial freedom. Perhaps even more important is the ability to practice discernment. Discernment is simply the process of making a good decision, especially when the answer to the question you are facing isn't immediately clear. When you are presented with an opportunity, such as a new job or the chance to start a new business, there are strategies that you can use to find clarity when the answer isn't immediately clear.

Here are some different ways that you can practice discernment when facing difficult decisions:

- **Don't Listen to Everyone** – Not everyone that gives you advice has your best interests in mind. When someone offers you advice, ask yourself what qualifications they have to give you advice and what might be in it for them if you take their advice. Some people just like to give advice so that they feel helpful, even if they have no idea what they are talking about. Focus on getting advice from people with no vested interest in the decision you make and from people that have specialized knowledge regarding the decision you are making.

- **Build a Circle of Trust** – Make a list of friends and business acquaintances that genuinely have your best interests in mind. When making a big decision, run the idea past them so that you can get advice from multiple perspectives. Your judgment can sometimes be clouded when agonizing over a decision, and trusted friends and family members can often see things that you can't. The Bible says that "plans fail for lack of counsel, but with many advisers they succeed" (Proverbs 15:22).

- **Let Your Subconscious Do the Thinking** – Your brain has the ability to continue to process and make neural connections even when you are not actively thinking about an issue. When facing a challenging question, go for a walk or sleep on it and the answer to your question may become clear to you.

- **Take The Long View** – Instead of asking yourself, "What should I do now?" ask yourself, "In five years, is this the choice I would have made, or would I have chosen something else?" This will shift you from short-term thinking to long-term thinking and will encourage you to make a decision that might be hard now, but is better for you over the long term.

- **Take Yourself Out of the Situation** – Sometimes we get mired in our own emotions when making decisions. Pretend that a friend of yours is making the same decision that you are facing. What advice would you offer to your friend? How would your advice to a friend be different than the advice that you give to yourself?

- **Gather More Information** – When evaluating a new job or business opportunity, you are often asked to make a decision that will affect the next several years of your life based on a handful of conversations. If you find yourself in a situation where you don't have enough information to make a decision, go out and seek the information you need. For a career decision, this might mean talking to other people that work for the new company you are considering or doing online research about the company.

- **Use a Decision Matrix** – A decision matrix is a spreadsheet that will help you weigh a variety of considerations when making a decision between multiple potential choices. It is effectively a pros and cons list on steroids. Lifehacker has put together an easy-to-use decision matrix spreadsheet, located at http://bit.ly/lifehackerdecisionmatrix.

Practicing discernment will be increasingly important as you begin to build wealth. You will have to make many tough decisions about what projects you want to pursue and who you want to share your wealth with. Once word gets out that you are someone with significant financial resources, people will come looking for your wealth, your advice and your partnership. Many of the requests that you receive will be easy noes, but other times the answer won't be so clear. You may genuinely want to help out a friend in need, only to realize that giving them money might not actually be helping them. You might want to help out a nonprofit, but be unsure about whether or not they are spending money effectively. You might be presented with a great job offer or business opportunity that has a substantial upfront cost which would prevent you from pursuing other projects. When situations like these arise, lean on the strategies above to make wise decisions.

Not every decision that you make will be perfect. You will probably make a lot of mistakes along your journey to wealth, and that's entirely okay. I have made more than my fair share of mistakes. I have made bad investments, given money to ineffective charities, launched businesses that have gone nowhere and have done business with people I regret going into business with. The key to making better decisions in the future is to learn from the mistakes that you have made in the past. Take time to evaluate bad decisions, understand why you made the decision that you did and what you would do differently the next time around.

My Lifelong Learning Plan

Take a moment to create a plan about how you will add life-long learning to your daily routine. You might want to start reading regularly or listening to audiobooks. You might subscribe to educational or business podcasts. You might take an online course or take a class at a local community college. Write down a list of actionable things that you can regularly do to increase your education over time.

I will do the following things to embark on a path of lifelong learning:

_____

_____

_____

_____

_____

_____

_____

_____

_____

_____

_____

_____

_____

_____

Wrap-up

Your long-term career and financial success will depend on your ability to increase the amount of value that you provide to the marketplace over time. If you know things that other people don't know, you will be able to do things that other people cannot do. In other words, you will be able to do more and create more economic value if you know more than everyone else. By setting out on a path of lifelong learning and learning how to effectively practice discernment, you will have the wisdom to build wealth and the wisdom to keep it and use it wisely after you have earned it.

Action Steps

- [ ] Develop an automatic learning habit, such as reading 20 minutes per day before bed.

- [ ] Determine to have a dynamic view of your identity and begin to identify what kind of person you would like to become over the next five to ten years.

- [ ] Review whether services like Udemy, Lynda, or Audible would accelerate your lifelong learning efforts.

- [ ] Develop an automatic learning habit, such as reading 20 minutes per day before bed.

- [ ] Use the discernment strategies outlined in this chapter when facing a difficult decision.

Intermission

Building wealth is a marathon process that can easily span a decade or more. While the skills that you need to build wealth over time are relatively straightforward, applying them consistently can be much more difficult. As much as I would like to offer you the "little known secrets of the rich" in this book, they do not actually exist. If you are reading this book to find an easy way to build wealth and get rich, you're probably starting to feel disappointed. Building wealth takes a substantial amount of time and energy and there is no step-by-step plan for you to follow, because every wealthy person's journey is different.

Remember that wealth is created by selling goods and services that other people find valuable enough to trade their hard-earned money for. As you generate value in the marketplace by educating yourself while leveraging opportunities that allow you to maximize your own and your business' value, your income will rise and you will be capable of building wealth.

At this point in the book, you should have created your dream spending plan and a long term savings goal that serves as your finish line for wealth building. You should also have the outline of your dream career plan created and some goals to help you move in that direction. Your dream career plan will allow you to increase your income over time so that you have the capacity to build wealth. You should also have begun to identify personal networking opportunities so that business and career opportunities show up at your doorstep. Further, you should have begun to put habits in place that will set you on a path of lifelong learning so that you can become more valuable over time.

The first half of the book contains what you need to know in order to create value and increase your income. In the second half of the book, we will focus entirely on how to manage your money. Earning a great income won't be enough to build wealth unless you also know how to manage the money that comes in. You would be surprised how many doctors and lawyers live paycheck-to-paycheck because they don't know how to manage their money. They often have six figures in student loan debt right out of school and end up purchasing cars and homes that they can't afford because they believe they can afford them based on their career choice.

In the remainder of the book, I will teach you how to manage and invest your money. We will go over some of the more fundamental topics such as budgeting, credit and debt, so you don't get stuck in the traps that affluent people often find themselves in. We will also examine more advanced topics like investing for lifetime income, minimizing your tax burden, and effectively giving to charities. I won't beat you over the head with absolute basics of personal finance. I also won't waste your time with a bunch of mushy stories that tug on your heartstrings but don't actually provide any practical guidance. Rather, you will learn how to effectively direct your money so that you can avoid the perils of debt, create a lifetime income, reduce the likelihood of getting sued, minimize your tax burden and do good work in the world through the power of charitable giving.

Chapter Five:
Creating a Monthly
Spending Plan

Let's face it. Nobody likes budgeting. Budgets are boring. Budgets tend to take a lot of work to put together on a monthly basis. It's often hard to get the numbers right for the first few months of budgeting. They can be hard to follow if you have never lived off of a budget before. Worst of all, budgets constrain your ability to spend money and have fun. In the short term, it would be much more enjoyable to just forget about budgeting altogether and spend what you want on whatever you want. However, we're not looking for short-term enjoyment. We are playing a much longer game that will enable us to build wealth over the course of the next ten years. If you want to build wealth, you are going to need to save and invest a significant portion of your income every month. The best way to make sure that saving and investing for the future remains a priority in your financial life is to create a monthly spending plan and stick to it.

When many people think of budgeting, they think of complicated spreadsheets, managing check registers or putting cash into envelopes. While this is how most people did budgeting twenty years ago, there are much better ways to budget today. There are tools that will help you develop a spending plan in less than an hour and will automatically track and categorize spending from your credit or debit card. If you spend more than twenty minutes per week thinking about your budget, you're doing it wrong. In the remainder of this chapter, I'll show you how to create a budget that actually works, is easy to manage, and will enable you to put a financial margin in your life so that you have the ability to save and invest in the future.

What is a Budget?

Budgeting is simply developing a plan that will determine how you spend your monthly income. In other words, a budget is merely a monthly spending plan. In order to create your budget, make a list of the income sources that you expect to receive income from next month and total the amount you expect to accumulate. Include every source of income in that number, including your salary, money from any businesses that you own, cash from part-time jobs and any investment income.

Once you know how much you can spend each month, make a list of spending categories and determine how much money you want to spend in each category every month.

When I put together a budget, I always put charitable giving and investing at the top of the budget so that they remain the priority in my life. I then list out all of my basic living expenses, including housing, food, utilities, and transportation. Next, I include insurance and any other recurring bills that need to be paid every month.

At the bottom of the budget, I list categories that are more wants than needs, like the large bills I rack up with Amazon for books each month. The general rule of thumb is that the highest priority categories are listed first to ensure that they actually get funded in your budget.

The total amount of money that you allocate to your spending categories should match the amount of income that you earn each month. Every dollar that you earn should be in a category in the budget so that there aren't any extra dollars floating around your bank account that don't have a plan attached to them.

When the month you are budgeting for begins, commit to only spend what you have decided ahead of time. If the money isn't in your budget, don't spend it. If there's something you absolutely have to spend money on, you'll have to adjust your budget and take money out of another category so that you can pay for the unbudgeted expense that came up.

Keep track of your spending to make sure that you don't spend excessively in any category using a spreadsheet or online budgeting tools.

If you can stay within the spending limits for each category that you created, you have successfully lived on a budget. When the end of the month comes around, set up the following month's budget so that you are ready for the next month's budget on the first of the month.

It takes time to budget effectively. For the first few months, you will find yourself constantly adjusting what you put in each of your categories because you probably do not know what you spend each month. After you have gone through two or three budgeting cycles, you will learn what you generally spend in different areas and the process will become more natural to you.

Why Create a Monthly Budget?

Your budget is the tool that enables you to use your money to achieve your financial goals. When you don't have a monthly budget in place, you are naturally inclined to spend money freely and hand over your credit card whenever there is something you want to do that requires money. Working toward long-term financial goals doesn't come naturally to most people.

You probably won't achieve your financial goals unless you have a month-by-month plan to work toward them. Your budget is that plan. A budget will shift your spending from what feels good now toward what will be best for you and your family in the future.

Budgets also enforce financial discipline in your life. When you aren't keeping track of what you spend, it can be very easy to spend more than you make each month without even realizing it. You may put all of your expenses on a credit card every month, pay some of it off each month but never quite get back to zero. Over time, your spending and interest charges add up and you have a large mess of a credit card debt to deal with.

When you have a budget in place, you immediately know when your spending has outpaced your income in a month and can take action to correct that issue.

Online Budgeting Tools

When I first started budgeting, I used the envelope system, which involved putting cash in categorized envelopes. It didn't take long for me to realize that putting cash in envelopes probably wasn't going to work well in a society that primarily uses debit and credit cards to make payments. I briefly toyed with downloadable budgeting software and then transitioned into using a spreadsheet that I put together from a template I found online. I used that spreadsheet for many years until I realized that web-based budgeting systems are really the best way for anyone to budget in the 21st century.

Web-based budgeting software tools have gotten so good that if you are going to put together your first budget, you would need an extremely compelling reason not to use a tool like Mint.com or YouNeedABudget.com. These tools will provide you with a step-by-step process to create your first budget and then will automatically track your spending to show how close you are to the plan that you created on their website or app.

Online budgeting tools can help you out in a number of different ways as well. Here are some other features and benefits that are common in web-based budgeting tools like Mint.com:

- Receive a free copy of your credit score and credit report.
- Get automatic alerts when bills become due.
- Track your investments and your personal net worth.
- Receive alerts when large transactions happen in your account.
- Develop savings goals for specific purchases.

- Automatically sync with your credit cards and bank accounts.
- Receive an automatic weekly summary of how you are doing compared to your budget.
- Access your budget from a mobile app.

Here are some of the most popular online budgeting tools:

- Mint.com (mint.com)
- YouNeedABudget (youneedabudget.com)
- Every Dollar (everydollar.com)
- Budget Simple (budgetsimple.com)
- LevelMoney (levelmoney.com)
- Mvelopes (mvelopes.com)

Can I Trust Web-Based Budgeting Tools?

Many people wonder if online budgeting tools are secure and safe to use. No one would want to connect their bank account to an online budgeting tool if there was a chance that their financial accounts could be compromised or stolen.

There is risk of identity theft whenever you make a payment with a credit card in person or online—that's just the reality of the world that we live in. When a major retailer's database gets breached, they send you a form letter and you probably continue to shop there.

If Mint.com's security was breached, you would close your account immediately and never use them again. They would be out of business overnight. Mint.com and their competitors know this and are working around the clock to make sure that your financial data is safe. As someone with a computer science and web security background, I have personally trusted my financial data with multiple well-known online financial tracking tools like Mint.com.

Granted, I probably wouldn't hook my bank account up to a website that I had never heard of before. But when it comes to well-known tools like Credit Karma, Mint and Personal Capital, I have no hesitation or concern about their security practices or the safety of my financial accounts in their hands.

Budgeting with an Irregular Income

If you are an entrepreneur, a commission-based sales person or otherwise have an income that fluctuates from month to month, budgeting can be a more challenging task. When you aren't sure how much money is going to come in for any given month, prioritizing your budget becomes much more important.

If you have an irregular income, your expense categories should be listed from most important to least important. As money comes in throughout the month, you pay the most important categories first and keep working down the list of categories until you run out of money.

There might be some "would be nice" categories that you just don't get to if you have a month where your income is lower than usual. If you have a better than average month, you can fully fund all of the categories in your budget and do a separate spending plan for any money that comes in on top of your normal budget amount.

Another strategy for dealing with an irregular income is setting up a separate savings account called a "leveling fund" that helps smooth out the amount of income you make each month. First, try to determine what your average income has been each month over the last year. Use that as the baseline for how much you should allocate to spend in your monthly budget.

If you have a better than average month, stick the extra income into the leveling fund and only live off of your 12-month average income. When you have a month where your income falls below your 12-month average, you can dip into the leveling fund so that you can continue to spend your average income.

Budgeting Extra Money

Every now and then you may find yourself with some extra money that you weren't planning on getting. You might have put in some extra hours at work, earned some money doing a gig on weekends, or received some money for your birthday. When extra money shows up, you should put it toward your next financial goal.

Maybe you want to pay off a debt, build your emergency fund or work on maxing out your Roth IRA. You should always have an idea in the back of your mind of where you are going to put any extra money that comes in, so that you're prepared if you get an extra few hundred dollars in a month. If some kind of major financial windfall comes your way, such as a large bonus or an inheritance, let it sit in a savings account for at least 30 days before doing anything with it. I would consider a financial windfall anything more than the equivalent of one month of your income.

Financial windfalls don't happen very often and nobody would want to look back a year down the road and realize that they squandered an opportunity. You wouldn't want to go out and buy something expensive that you would normally never buy and look back at that purchase with regret when the money runs out.

Before doing anything with it, take some time and really think about what the best use of that money would be. A couple of years ago, I received a six-figure payout from the sale of part of my business. I left that money in my savings account for 90 days before deciding to put some toward taxes, some toward giving, and investing the remainder in the market.

Budgeting Alone Won't Make You Wealthy

I believe that everyone should create a budget and track their spending, because it allows you to know with certainty that you are living on less than you make and that your spending patterns are in alignment with your long-term financial goals. However, creating a monthly spending plan alone won't automatically make you wealthy over a long period of time. You can be the best money manager in the world, but if you don't make much money and have a lot of fixed monthly expenses, you are never going to become wealthy. Budgeting alone simply can't make you wealthy.

If you want to build long-term wealth, you will have to significantly increase your income using the strategies outlined in Chapter 2 of this book. By earning a large income and living off a fraction of what you make each month, you will have hundreds or even thousands of dollars left over at the end of every month, which you can use to invest for your future needs.

Don't Skip the Latte

Many personal finance authors tell their readers to cut out their morning latte, quit smoking or stop going out for lunch every day so that they can save an extra $5 or $10 per day.

They show how a little bit of money saved every month can add up to a lot of money over the course of a couple of decades. Let's say that you actually took this advice and stopped getting a $4 latte on the way to work every morning. You would be able to save around $80 per month. If you did this for ten years and actually invested the money, you would have around $15,000 in your investment account if the market returned around its historical averages. I don't know about you, but I would get a lot more joy out of having a latte every morning for ten years than having $15,000 in a savings account ten years from now.

When putting your budget together, the goal shouldn't be to cut everything fun out of your life so that you can put a little bit extra away each month. The goal should be to develop a sustainable long-term financial plan that you can actually live on. If you can't easily afford a morning trip to Starbucks or can't afford to go out to lunch with some friends as part of your monthly budget, you have a problem with your income, not your budget. If your small daily enjoyments can't fit into your budget, look for ways to increase your income rather than simply trying to eliminate them from your life.

My Budgeting Plan

Take a moment to write down how you plan on putting your budget together. What date will you begin living on a budget? What tool(s) are you going to use to create your budget and track your spending each month? How are you going to make sure that you are on track with your budget? How are you going to make sure that saving, investing and charitable giving remain a priority in your budget?

_____

_____

_____

_____

_____

_____

_____

_____

_____

_____

_____

_____

_____

_____

Budgeting When You're Wealthy

When you begin earning more than six figures each year, budgeting starts looking a lot different for you than it does for most people. Unless you're living a really expensive lifestyle, there is probably not much of a concern about whether or not your bills are going to get paid each month. I still generally recommend that wealthy people do a budget, but the actual layout of the budget can look a lot simpler. My wife and I currently only have five categories in our monthly budget, because we know that all of the bills are going to get paid every month and that we will still have quite a bit left over, even if we exceed our budget and spend more than we are planning to in any given month. For wealthy people, budgeting is much more about tracking your total spending every month—making sure that you can save, give and invest the dollars that you want—than it is about making sure that the most important bills actually get paid. As a wealthy person, having a plan will ensure that you don't outspend your income and will make sure that you can still hit your major financial goals.

As you begin to build wealth, you will notice that your time is more limited. When you create a lot of economic value in the world, there will be more demands placed on your time. People who are becoming wealthy tend to do a lot more and be a lot more active in the community than those that aren't. They also have greater demands placed on them at their job or their businesses. When you become wealthy, your budget should reflect this reality.

As you begin to build wealth, there are some things that it just doesn't make sense for you to do anymore. If you make $200,000 per year, your time is worth $100 per hour (assuming you work 40 hours per week for 50 weeks each year). If you find yourself doing a bunch of $20 an hour tasks around your house at the expense of creating economic value in your job or your business, you should hire out that work to someone else. For example, it rarely makes sense for wealthy people to do their own lawn care, snow removal and house cleaning. Periodically ask yourself what tasks you should stop doing and start hiring out, and then integrate those costs into your monthly budget.

The Lifestyles of the Rich and Famous

If you begin to do really well in life and are earning six figures a few times over, you are going to have to seriously consider what kind of lifestyle you want to live. Do you want to drive a Ferrari, live in a million-dollar-plus home on the edge of a lake or a golf course and show off your wealth on every possible occasion? Or would you rather live a more upper-middle-class lifestyle? You might get slightly more enjoyment out of having a big house and buying a lot of really nice stuff, or you might feel better about spending less, not showing your wealth to the world and having more money to give and invest.

My wife and I have intentionally chosen not to live a "millionaire lifestyle" for a few different reasons. We have a nice house and both drive relatively new Hondas, but you won't see us flashing money around or purchasing really expensive stuff just because we can. We've decided that we're happy where we are at and believe that a nicer house, nicer cars and fancier stuff won't make us any happier than we are today. We also want our children to grow up in a normal home with normal stuff so that they don't become spoiled, entitled, and think that they should be able to have everything they want. Finally, we get much more joy out of building wealth and giving to charity than we do from having nicer stuff.

I don't advocate extreme frugality, but I do think there is an upper limit to the amount of joy that you can receive from having a nicer lifestyle. Owning a Porsche or a Mercedes-Benz probably won't make you any happier than driving a Honda or a Toyota. Remember that your personal happiness comes from within and not from having nicer stuff. You also introduce a new set of problems when everyone knows that you're wealthy and you're not afraid to show it off. As we discussed in Chapter 1, if everyone knows that you have money, there are going to be people that try to get your money. It can also be a lot of work to manage all of your stuff when you have a luxurious lifestyle. You might need to hire people, like a maid and a gardener, just to maintain your house. There's something to be said for living a simpler lifestyle and not having to keep track of or worry about all of your stuff.

Wrap-up

While most people have negative preconceptions about budgets, creating and following a budget doesn't have to be hard or time-consuming. By using modern web-based budgeting tools and a little bit of discipline, you can create and track your budget in an hour or two each month. With your budget in place, you can make sure that you are working toward your long-term financial goals and are not spending more than you make each month.

Action Steps

☐ Commit to creating a personal budget each and every month.

☐ Select what online budgeting software you want to use.

☐ Create your first monthly budget.

Chapter Six:
Credit and Debt

If there's a topic that divides personal finance authors more than anything, it's debt. On one side of the debate, Dave Ramsey and his followers abhor the use of debt in every circumstance. He recommends that people don't use credit cards, pay no attention to their credit score and pay cash in every circumstance. He even suggests that his followers try to save up and pay cash for their first home if they can swing it. On the other side, there are authors like Robert Kiyosaki and Pamela Yellen who advocate strategies like buying rental real estate with no money down and borrowing from whole life insurance policies as core aspects of one's personal finance strategy. To them, debt is a tool that lets people leverage other people's money to create wealth. While the debate over debt's supposed necessity versus its damaging effects rages on, I believe that the proper use of debt lies between these two extremes.

Americans Love Debt

People in the United States love to take on debt. We borrow through credit cards, mortgages, payday loans, home equity loans, personal loans, in-store credit, student loans, car loans, title loans and many other financial products to pay for just about everything. The typical American family now has an average of $15,355 of credit card debt and average total debt of $129,579 (http://nerdwallet.com/blog/credit-card-data/average-credit-card-debt-household). 72.1% of Americans have at least one credit card, and 16% of Americans have at least five credit cards (http://creditcards.com/credit-card-news/ownership-statistics-charts-1276.php). 80% of all Americans are in debt of one kind or another. Companies make it very easy for us to sign up for debt and many Americans are more than happy to use the credit that's made available to them.

Want to Become Wealthy? Avoid Debt.

While taking on a manageable level of debt to purchase a home or fund your education can be a good idea, many people take on far too much debt. When you have a lot of consumer debt, it is very difficult to become wealthy because of the interest payments you have to make each month. If you have $50,000 in credit card debt at a 15% APY, you are paying $625 per month in interest to service that debt. That's $625 every month that can't go toward reducing debt, can't be put away in savings and can't be invested for the future.

Albert Einstein is reported to have said that "Compound interest is the most powerful force in the universe." When you invest your money in stocks and bonds, the power of compound interest works in your favor. You receive interest and capital appreciation on your investments regularly and over time the value of your investments will grow exponentially. When you borrow money, compound interest is working against you. You are being charged interest each month for the privilege of borrowing someone else's money. The interest charges that you pay on your personal debt make it harder for you to get out of debt, because a major portion of your payment isn't going toward reducing your principal balance.

Wealthy people recognize the true cost of borrowing through consumer debt and generally avoid it. A while back, Forbes undertook a survey of the 400 wealthiest Americans. When asked about wealth building, a whopping 75% of them said the best way to build wealth is to become and stay debt-free (https://daveramsey.com/blog/7-characteristics-of-debt-free-people). If you want to become financially independent over the course of the next decade, you should take the advice of the Forbes 400 and work to eliminate any personal debt that you carry.

I personally have no debt to my name. My wife and I own our home free and clear and have paid cash for both vehicles we own. We do use credit cards, but pay them off in full every month. All of my businesses are funded entirely out of operations and we do not use debt in any part of our business. I have personally taken out a student loan and a mortgage on my home, but I paid both off as quickly as I possibly could. My wife and I have not had any personal debt since we paid off the mortgage on our current home more than three years ago.

"Good Debt" and "Bad Debt"

A lot of personal finance authors will break down debt into "good debt" that's tied to an appreciating asset—like a home, a business or a college education—and "bad debt" that's used to finance a depreciating asset like credit cards, payday loans and car loans. While some types of debt are certainly worse than others, I don't think any debt should be characterized as "good debt."

Calling any kind of debt "good debt" encourages people to borrow money that they might otherwise not borrow and minimizes the perception of risk that's associated with debt. I like to think of mortgages, student loans and other types of "good debt" as "necessary evil debt." It's not the worst thing in the world to buy a home with a mortgage, use a student loan to help pay for college or get financing for your business, but you should always minimize the amount of money that you borrow and try to get the most favorable terms you can.

Here are some considerations for the various types of "good debt" that you may want to use:

- **Mortgages** – Most people will need to take out a mortgage to pay for their first home. With interest rates near historic lows, it may be tempting to borrow more than you might otherwise. Keep your mortgage payment under 25% of your take-home pay so that your mortgage payment doesn't consume too much of your monthly income. If at all possible, get a 15-year fixed-rate loan. Your payment will be slightly higher than a 30-year loan, but you'll shave a full fifteen years of payments off your mortgage.

- **Student Loans** – If you are going to borrow money for college, make sure that your degree is preparing you for a career that will enable you to pay off your student loan debt. Only borrow money through the federal student loan program and avoid private loans like the plague. Never borrow more for your education than you expect to earn in your career in the first year after you graduate. I also strongly recommend attending an in-state public university to reduce the cost of your education. Attending more expensive private schools almost never makes sense from a financial perspective.

- **Business Debt** – While avoiding business debt is preferable, it may be necessary to take on debt depending on the type of business that you have. For example, you might need some short-term financing to pay for inventory, which can be repaid when you receive orders from your customers. Avoid financing your regular operating expenses through a line of credit or a credit card. Your regular operating expenses should always be funded out of cash flow. If you have to dip into a credit card to make payroll or cover another regular expense, you're headed for trouble.

- **Debt Consolidation Loans** – If you are working to reduce your debt, you may be able to use a debt consolidation loan to lower the amount of interest that you pay on your debt. Taking out a debt consolidation loan will only work if you stop borrowing money. If you keep racking up credit card debt after taking out a debt consolidation loan, you will only make your debt problem worse. Never use a home equity loan for debt consolidation, because that turns unsecured debt into foreclosure debt if you aren't able to make your payment.

Here are some types of debt that you should generally avoid:

- **Auto Loans** – Buying a car, especially a new one, can be an incredibly expensive proposition. It just doesn't make sense to pay interest for the privilege of owning an asset that's going down in value. Pay cash for a used car if at all possible. If you can't afford to buy a vehicle with cash, purchase the least expensive reliable vehicle you can and pay it off as soon as possible.

- **Payday Loans** – These short term loans prey upon low-income consumers and charge annualized interest rates of 400% or more. No one should ever take out a payday loan under any circumstances.

- **In-Store Financing and Store Credit Cards** – There's a reason that every major department store asks you if you want to sign up for their credit card at checkout. Store credit cards are a great deal for retailers and a horrible deal for consumers. Store credit cards have much higher interest rates than regular credit cards. These cards also come with very unfavorable terms and often do not offer any rewards. You are almost always better off paying for purchases with your own credit cards.

- **Credit Cards** – It's totally okay to make purchases with a credit card, just be sure to pay off the balance each and every month. Because you never earn a return on your purchases, credit card debt falls into the "bad debt" category. Credit cards also have higher interest rates than other types of loans and your debt level may rise over time if you only make the minimum payment.

- **IRS Debt** – If there's anyone that you don't want to owe money to, it's the Internal Revenue Service. They should always get paid first after taking care of the basic necessities of life. If you don't file your taxes or simply fail to pay them, you'll be hit with additional fees and penalties that add up quickly. The IRS can also place liens on your home and any other assets that you might have.

- **Home Equity Loans** – Home equity loans can offer very attractive interest rates, but they also put your home at risk. As with a mortgage, your lender can foreclose on your home if you fail to make the payments. It rarely makes sense to put your home at risk for the privilege of borrowing money, so I generally recommend avoiding home equity loans.

With so many creative financing options entering the market, there are simply too many types of "bad debt" loans to list. These include signature loans, personal loans from a bank, pawn shop loans, title loans, and appliance loans. These loans should also be avoided. If at all possible, only borrow for the four categories of "necessary evil" debt that I listed in the previous section. For everything else, save up and pay cash for your purchases.

Remember that every additional loan that you sign up for adds one more mandatory monthly payment to your budget, reducing your ability to save and invest toward your long-term savings goal. If you want to achieve financial freedom, debt should not be a regular part of your life. Become and stay debt-free so that you can save and invest more money each month and reach your goal of financial freedom faster.

If You Have a Lot of Debt...

If you are deeply in debt or are behind on your bills, you can still begin your ten-year turnaround even though you'll be starting from behind. I truly believe that anyone can dramatically transform their finances over the course of ten years, regardless of where they are starting at. When I began my ten-year turnaround, I had credit cards and student loan debt to deal with. I was able to pay those off during the first two years of my turnaround and have since gone on to build a significant amount of wealth.

If you are in debt, follow the instructions in Chapters 1-4 to increase your income over time and begin living on a budget. With a larger income and a spending plan in place, it will be much easier for you to pay off your debt. If you're not sure how to get out of debt, go pick up Dave Ramsey's *The Total Money Makeover* book and sign up for a Financial Peace University class. Dave Ramsey's material is highly motivating and offers a step-by-step plan that anyone can use to get out of debt. Dave Ramsey teaches a strategy called the "debt snowball" which involves paying off debts from smallest to largest. You can learn more about snowballing debt at http://daveramsey.com/blog/how-the-debt-snowball-method-works. Once you have worked through your debt, your monthly cash flow will be freed up and you can begin to apply the investing and wealth building strategies outlined in Chapter 7 of this book.

My Personal Debt Commitment

I, _____ (your name), hereby promise to borrow as little as possible during my ten-year turnaround.

I recognize that having debt will severely hinder my ability to build wealth and attain financial freedom.

I will only take on debt for the purchase of a reasonable home and for my education if absolutely necessary.

I will pay off my credit cards each and every month.

I promise to get and stay out of debt so that compound interest is working for me and not against me.

I will not get a car loan, a payday loan, a store credit card, in-store financing, a home equity loan, a personal loan or any other type of debt for any purpose under any circumstances. Period.

_____
signature

_____
date

A Note for Christians About Debt

The Bible does not explicitly endorse or forbid a Christian from borrowing money, but it does offer explicit instructions for Christians who are in debt. The Apostle Paul wrote in the book of Romans that we should "let no debt remain outstanding, except the continuing debt to love one another, for whoever loves others has fulfilled the law" (Romans 13:8). The Book of Psalms echoes the Christian's responsibility to repay debt: "The wicked borrow and do not repay, but the righteous give generously" (Psalm 37:21).

If you are a Christian who is in debt, work diligently to get out of debt so that there is nothing hampering your ability to answer God's calling on your life. The Bible says that a borrower becomes a servant to their lender (Proverbs 22:7). Jesus said "No one can serve two masters. Either you will hate the one and love the other, or you will be devoted to the one and despise the other. You cannot serve both God and money" (Matthew 6:24).

When you have to service a large amount of debt, you may not be able to be obedient to God's calling. What if God were to call you to give to a specific cause? What if he were to call you to serve as a short-term missionary or work in a ministry job? Would you be able to afford to say "yes" to the call that God places on your life? If the answer is "no," begin working to get out of debt so that you can respond to any call God challenges you with.

The Proper Use of Credit Cards

Carrying a balance on a credit card is never a good idea, but that doesn't mean you should avoid using credit cards altogether. If you see credit cards as "free money" or otherwise regularly find yourself carrying a balance, don't use credit cards. The interest charges you will pay each month will negate any of the benefits of using a credit card. But if you can pay off your credit card every month like clockwork, there are some financial benefits to paying for purchases with a credit card.

Here are some reasons that you might want to pay for your purchases with a credit card:

- **Rewards** – There are multiple credit cards that will give you 2% cash back. Using one of these credit cards is tantamount to getting a 2% discount on every purchase that you make. If you put $5,000 on your credit card each month, that's $100 in free cash that you wouldn't otherwise have received. As of mid-2016, the best cash-back rewards credit card is the "Citi Double Cash" card, which effectively pays 2% cash back on all purchases. These offers tend to change over time, so visit websites like NerdWallet.com and CreditCards.com to find the best current offer. If you travel frequently, you may be able to leverage rewards to get even more than 2% cash back in travel. Visit thepointsguy.com and abroaders.com for resources on travel rewards for credit cards.

- **Chargeback Rights** – If you have a problem with a purchase or if something you order online doesn't show up, you have the right to file a chargeback within 60 days of the purchase with your credit card company. More often than not, the credit card company will side with you over a merchant because you're their customer.

- **Fraud Protection** – If your credit card is ever lost or stolen, you are not responsible for any fraudulent charges that are made under your card. You just have to call your credit card company, who will cancel the charges and issue you a new card. If your debit card is stolen, your checking account will get wiped out. Then you'll have to fight with your bank to get your own money back. For this reason alone, it's much better to pay for purchases with a credit card than a debit card.

- **Travel Benefits** – Many credit cards offer a number of additional benefits for travelers, such as rental car insurance, trip cancellation insurance, lost luggage reimbursement and roadside assistance. A few cards will even get you into airport lounges for free.

- **Purchase Protection Benefits** – Many credit cards will extend a manufacturer's warranty by another 12 months and will offer you price protection if something you buy goes down in price.

I truly believe that using a credit card is the best way to make purchases, as long as you have the discipline to only purchase what's within your budget and to pay off your balance each month. Between my business and personal purchases, I earned more than $10,000 in credit card rewards in 2015. I was able to use those rewards to send my parents to Las Vegas for a week (http://bit.ly/matt-points-and-miles) and attend a number of conferences without having to pay for airfares or a hotel. I've been able to use airport lounges for free and have gotten reimbursed after an airline couldn't find my luggage. I can't count how many times that chargeback rights and fraud protection have saved the day from misbehaving merchants and fraudulent charges. While paying with a credit card won't get you dramatically closer to financial freedom than paying with cash or a debit card, the rewards, additional perks and fraud protection make credit cards my preferred payment method.

Building Your Credit

If your credit score is already in good shape, feel free to skip over this section. If you have bad credit or have never established credit before, there are concrete action steps that you can take to start building or rebuilding your credit score. If you have never taken out a loan before and want to start building your credit, your first step is to visit a local credit union and ask if opening a checking or savings account will allow you to participate in a "fresh start" program that provides a credit card without a credit history check. Alternatively, you can sign up for a secured credit card, which requires a cash collateral deposit that becomes the credit line for that account. For example, if you deposit $500 into a collateral account, you will have a credit limit of $500. Use your new credit card sparingly and pay off the balance each month. The credit card company will report your payment history to the three major credit bureaus and your score will rise over time as you establish a track record of on-time payments.

If you have bad credit, you have probably noticed ads from companies that will promise to fix your credit or help you establish a new credit identity. Many of these offers are outright scams.

If any company promises that they can remove accurate negative information from your report, requires you to pay up front or suggests that they can get you a new credit identity, run in the opposite direction. You are better off repairing your credit yourself by working through and settling any bad debt that you may have, fixing erroneous information on your credit report and establishing a record of on-time payments in the future. While there is no quick fix for bad credit, FICO has produced a guide that provides tips to improve your credit score over time, located at http://myfico.com/crediteducation/improveyourscore.aspx.

Protecting Your Credit

The information on your credit report is now used for applications beyond whether or not you are approved for a loan. Even if you never plan to borrow money again, you should still regularly monitor your credit report because your credit score is used by insurance companies, cell phone carriers, apartment complexes, utility providers and many other companies. You should also monitor credit so that you can spot any fraudulent accounts that have been created in your name by identity thieves.

Here are the three steps that I believe everyone should follow to protect their credit:

- **Freeze Your Credit** – The best way to stop identity thieves in their tracks is to put a security freeze on your credit reports with the three major bureaus— Equifax, TransUnion and Experian. A security freeze will prevent anyone from applying for credit in your name. If you need to apply for credit, you can temporarily lift the security freeze for 30 days so that a company can check your credit. While freezing your credit can create a bit of hassle when you want to apply for a loan down the line, the $30 you'll have to pay to freeze your credit is the cheapest form of identity theft insurance you can buy. Clark Howard has put together an excellent guide on freezing your credit located at http://clarkhoward.com/credit-freeze-and-thaw-guide. If you freeze your credit, make sure to write down the pin numbers that each of the bureaus give you and put them in a safe place. It can be very hard to unfreeze your credit file without having the pin numbers they give you.

- **Check Your Credit Reports Annually** – Every twelve months, you can check your credit reports from Equifax, TransUnion and Experian for free by visiting annualcreditreport.com. Annual Credit Report is a website that the three major bureaus were required to set up as part of the Fair Credit Reporting Act. At the same time every year, you should pull your credit reports to make sure they are accurate and that no fraudulent accounts are showing up on your credit report.

- **Get Free Credit Monitoring from Credit Karma** – Credit Karma is a website that provides you with free credit scores from TransUnion and Equifax, as well as free credit monitoring services that will alert you when changes are made to your credit reports. Like Mint.com, Credit Karma makes money by recommending credit cards, mortgages and other financial products. Because you can get completely free credit monitoring services from Credit Karma, it doesn't make sense to pay a monthly fee for credit monitoring services with another company.

If you find that an account has been opened in your name that you didn't authorize, you should take immediate action to resolve the matter. The FTC has put together an action guide on what you should do if your identity is stolen. The guide, titled "Taking Charge: What to Do if Your Identity Has Been Stolen" is located at https://consumer.ftc.gov/articles/pdf-0009-taking-charge.pdf.

Wrap-up

Debt can be an incredible barrier for anyone that wants to build wealth. If you are making large monthly payments to service debt, your ability to save and invest for the future is significantly diminished. Commit to minimizing any future borrowing and only borrow money for the purchase of a home, to fund your education (within reason) or to fund the growth of your business (if you have one). If you are in debt, use the "debt snowball" strategy to work through any debt that you have. Once you become debt-free, your monthly cash flow may be used to quickly build wealth using the strategies outlined in Chapter 7.

Action Steps

❑ Commit to minimize any future borrowing and commit to only borrow for your home, education or business.

❑ If you are in debt, use the "debt snowball" strategy to pay off any debt that you have.

❑ Freeze your credit report and set up free credit monitoring services through Credit Karma.

Chapter Seven: Investing and Wealth Building

Building wealth through investment will be both the easiest and hardest part of your ten-year turnaround. Developing and implementing a plan to build wealth and create a lifetime income is surprisingly easy, but there are many traps that can derail your efforts along the way. It will take many years for you to hit the long-term savings goal that will provide for your dream lifestyle.

You will be tempted to make decisions that are not in your best interest along the way. You might be tempted to pull your money out of the market during a recession, to move your money into a hot sector, or be wooed away from your strategy by a commission-based sales person who promises a bigger, better deal. The key to successful investing is developing a long-term plan, sticking to it and not letting market conditions cause you to make emotional trading decisions.

In this chapter, I'll show you how to avoid the most common traps that cause investors to lose money. You will learn an investment strategy that has historically outperformed the S&P 500 with lower volatility. You'll consider whether or not you should work with a financial advisor, how to minimize investment management fees that can kill your returns and how to use tax-deferred and tax-free accounts to keep the government off of your investment returns. Most importantly, you'll learn how to build an investment portfolio that will generate income every month so that you can eventually live entirely off of your investment income.

What Are We Trying to Accomplish?

The long-term goal for your investment portfolio should be to replace the income from your job with income that is generated by investments. When your investments throw off enough income to cover your monthly expenses—as defined by the dream spending plan you created in Chapter 1—you have achieved financial freedom. You will no longer need the income from your day job or your business to cover your expenses.

If you want to live off of $5,000 per month and you have investments that generate $5,000 per month, you can pretty much do whatever you want. You will have the complete and total freedom to quit working altogether, switch to a more enjoyable job or start the business you've always wanted to start. Any additional money that you earn after you've achieved financial freedom is pure gravy that you can give to charity, travel with or use to fund additional upgrades to your lifestyle.

Investment Trap #1: Emotional Buying and Selling

Before we dive into developing an investment strategy, we must first review the many different mistakes that investors make that cause their investments to underperform the broader stock market. By far the biggest mistake that investors make is emotional buying and selling. People buy when they should sell and sell when they should buy. When the market takes a dip, people sell their investments because they are afraid of losing more of their money. When the market is doing well, investors put more money into the market (often paying a premium for their investments) because they see that the market has been doing well recently.

Selling low and buying high has a huge negative impact on the returns that mutual fund investors receive. According to a Dalbar study, the average equity mutual fund investor underperformed the S&P 500 in 2014 by 8.19%. Mutual funds themselves posted an average return of 13.69%, but mutual fund investors only earned 5.50% on their money. The problem isn't that mutual funds are overstating their returns, but that mutual fund investors switch funds too often, buying when prices are high and selling when prices are low.

If you want to do well in the market over the long term, you have to learn to become impassive towards the volatility of the stock market and stick to the strategy that you start with. When you develop your asset allocation and long-term investment strategy, you need to plan to stick with that strategy for at least 5 years, hopefully even longer. Switching between strategies too often and buying and selling based on fear and greed are a recipe for dramatically underperforming in the market.

If you can't handle the swings of the stock market, you should probably hire a fee-only financial advisor to look after your money for you. A good financial advisor will be able to talk you down from the ledge when you're tempted to sell because of a bear market. Even though the financial advisor will take a 1% account management fee every year, that fee pales in comparison to the money that you can lose due to emotional buying and selling. I don't believe that everyone needs a financial advisor, but if you can't keep cool during a recession, you should hire a financial advisor to protect you from yourself.

Investment Trap #2: Investment Costs

Another common trap that causes investors to underperform the market is paying far more than they need to in fees, which significantly hampers the ability of compound interest to work in their favor.

Let's say that you invest in an S&P 500 index fund that has a management fee of 1% per year. While that doesn't sound like much, it can compound dramatically over time. You max out your Roth IRA each year from age 25 to age 65 and put your $5,500 annual investment into that mutual fund. If the mutual fund earns an average of 9% per year, you'll retire with about $1.6 million in the bank. If you were to make the same investments without the 1% annual fee from the mutual fund, you would have instead retired with $2.145 million. The 1% expense ratio charged by your mutual fund reduced your account returns by a whopping $545,000 over the course of your working lifetime. Because investment fees can dramatically reduce your returns, it's extremely important to know what fees you are paying and work to minimize those costs. Here are the types of fees that investors should watch out for:

- **Mutual Fund Operating Expenses** – Mutual fund operators charge a variety of annual management fees to invest in their funds. These annual fees can include management fees, 12b-1 or distribution (and/or service) fees and other expenses. These fees are often reported as an expense ratio, or the percentage of your assets in the fund that you will have to pay each year in fees. Mutual funds may have annual management fees that are as low as 0.05% and as high as 2.0% per year. If you invest in mutual funds, take time to look up the expense ratio of each fund you own. Compare the expense ratio of each fund to similar funds offered by Vanguard, Fidelity and T. Rowe Price. If you are paying dramatically more in fees than comparable funds offered by those three providers, consider switching to the lower cost option.

- **Sales Loads** – Some mutual funds charge a sales load, which serves as a commission for the financial professional selling the mutual fund to you. Sales loads can be charged at the time of purchase, known as a front-end load, or when you sell the mutual fund, known as a back-end load. As there is typically a "no load" equivalent to any load-charging mutual fund, I personally only purchase "no load" funds which do not charge a sales load.

- **Advisory Fees** – If you use a financial advisor to manage your investment portfolio, your advisor may charge you an ongoing annual fee based on the value of your portfolio. These fees can range from 0.5% on the low end to 2.5% on the high end. If you use a financial advisor, ask them what their annual management fee is. If your financial advisor charges an annual management fee of more than 1%, you should move your money to a less expensive advisor or manage your money yourself. See "Should I Use a Financial Advisor to Manage My Investments?" later in this chapter for more detail.

- **401(k) Fees** – Expenses for operating and administering a 401(k) plan are often passed along to its participants. These fees are charged in addition to the operating expenses of any mutual funds you hold inside of your 401(k) plan. These fees can vary significantly between different 401(k) providers. While it's good to be aware of any 401(k) fees you may be paying, you probably can't do much about the fees you are paying unless you can convince your employer to switch to a lower-cost provider.

- **Variable Annuity Fees** – Variable Annuities are very high-fee investment vehicles that are often promoted by commission-based salespeople. If you were to invest in a variable annuity, you will likely be charged an annual management fee to cover the expenses of a variable annuity, on top of the operating expenses that are held inside of any mutual funds that the variable annuity holds. If you want to get out of your variable annuity, you will likely be hit with a surrender charge that will vary based on how long you have owned the variable annuity. I do not recommend that anyone purchase a variable annuity under any circumstance because of the high fees that are charged by this type of investment vehicle.

- **Commissions** – You will pay a commission when you buy or sell a stock through a brokerage account or a financial professional. Most brokerage accounts charge less than $10 per trade. You can reduce those fees to as little as $2 if you are with the right low-cost broker and have a sufficiently large account.

Before buying a mutual fund or any other investment product, calculate the total fees that you will have to pay to make the investment. While there's no hard and fast rule about what is "too much" to pay in fees as a percentage of your investment, the lower you can get your investment fees, the better. Personally, I pay an average of less than 0.25% per year to maintain all of my investments. By not using a financial advisor for the bulk of my investments and investing primarily in low-cost index funds and individual stocks through Vanguard (a low-cost mutual fund provider), I have been able to pay dramatically less in both management fees and transaction fees than most investors.

Investment Trap #3: Investing in Tech Startups, Friends' Businesses and Private Equity Deals

I can't count how many times I've been asked to invest in the businesses of friends and acquaintances, private equity investments, tech startups, private loans and other complicated investment strategies. People in my community know that I'm a successful entrepreneur, and I get hit up for these types of things at least every other week. In many cases, someone believes they have the next big business idea and they just need a little bit of money to get started. Other times, a company is promoting a unique investment strategy, like investing in private mortgages, that promises better-than-market returns. These pitches tend to be alluring to investors, both because of the possibility of getting better returns and because it seems like it would be fun to share with friends and family about a great investment that you made.

While I have made a few small private equity investments, I generally say no to investments that promise better-than-market returns by default. While the initial pitch you receive might sound compelling, the actual mechanics of the deal are usually more trouble than they are worth. These types of investments are typically illiquid, have a lot more risk, and often involve complicated terms and conditions that can come back to bite you later. You typically won't know what the real risks of these types of investments are until you get into them.

If someone is coming to you for money, that probably means they have already tried and failed to get money from a bank or other investors. If the opportunity they were presenting to you as a small angel investor were really that great, a bank, an angel fund or a venture capital firm probably would have already written them a check. While some people make good money doing private equity deals and angel investments, it's usually not the person that has $25,000 or $50,000 to put into a business. Unless you plan on becoming a professional investor who knows the minute details of every deal that you participate in, you should probably stick to stocks, bonds, and real estate.

Investment Trap #4:
Investing in What You Don't Understand

A good rule of thumb is that you shouldn't invest in anything that you don't fully understand. If you don't know exactly how an investment instrument works, what you're investing in, why the investment will make money, what the expected returns are, what the investment costs are and what the potential risks are, you shouldn't invest your money. This is true for both investments that you might make in a business and for investments that a financial advisor or salesperson might try to pitch you.

If a financial salesperson is pitching you something that doesn't make sense to you, don't invest your money. If you're not 100% sure what you're signing up for, you risk getting stuck in an expensive investment vehicle that may be difficult to get out of down the line. If a salesperson is aggressively pushing you toward a financial product that you don't understand, it's probably because they are going to earn a big commission check for selling it to you. If the financial advisor doesn't do a great job of explaining what they're selling to you, you should find another advisor who can do a better job of educating you on investing.

Good investing should not be complicated. In fact, good investing is pretty boring. Effective investing usually just involves picking the right asset allocation of stocks and bonds, selecting low-cost mutual funds, regularly investing money every month and being smart enough to leave the money alone until you're financially free and want to start living off the income generated by your investments.

If you can do those things and avoid the traps of emotional buying and selling, regularly changing your strategy, paying too much in fees and buying things that you don't understand, your investments will significantly outperform those of most other investors.

Should I Use a Financial Advisor to Manage My Investments?

If personal finance and investing are a hobby for you and you want to spend time learning about asset allocation, researching mutual funds and keeping an eye on your accounts, you probably don't need a financial advisor.

Since you are currently reading a personal finance and personal development book, there's a pretty good chance that you fall into this category. If you're willing to do a little bit of research and legwork upfront, you can set up your own investment account with a brokerage like Vanguard, TD Ameritrade or Fidelity and develop an asset allocation very similar to what a financial advisor would set you up with, but at a significantly lower cost.

If your eyes glaze over whenever you try to read anything about investing, you will want to hire a financial advisor to manage your investments for you.

A financial advisor can help you select what type of retirement or other investment account is best for you, what kind of investment asset allocation is best for your situation, and keep you from making trades that are against your best interest when the market is down. Financial advisors generally won't be able to "beat the market," but they can make sure that you don't dramatically underperform the market, simply by making sure you're doing all of the right things.

As mentioned above, a financial advisor will usually charge an annual management fee of 0.5%-1% of your portfolio value each year. If your advisor charges more than 1% each year, you should switch to a lower-cost advisor.

If you are okay working with an advisor over phone and email, you can hire a personal financial advisor from Vanguard for a 0.3% annual management fee.

If you'd like to eliminate the human relationship component from your investment experience, you can use a robo-advisor like WealthFront or Betterment to manage your investments for you, for as little as 0.25% of your account per year. While you won't get the personal touch with a robo-advisor or an over-the-phone advisor, you can significantly reduce the cost of having someone manage your investments for you.

Financial advisors can do a number of other things besides managing your retirement investments. They can help you set up 529 college savings plans, charitable trusts and other unique investment account types. They can serve as a financial planner and make sure that you are on track to hit your long-term investment goals. They can also help you with your estate planning and help you put together wills, trusts and powers of attorney. Some financial advisors also work as independent insurance agents and can find the best deal on various types of insurance policies.

I don't personally use a financial advisor to manage the vast majority of my investments, but I do use a financial advisor for my "backdoor" Roth IRA, for a variety of insurance policies and for estate planning purposes. I have my advisor manage my Roth IRA because of the complexity of setting up an IRA when you are above the income limit. My advisor also has a much better beat on the insurance market than I do and does a great job of keeping an eye on my health insurance, life insurance and long-term disability insurance policies. I have also worked with an advisor to set up an estate plan for my family.

If you want to hire a financial advisor, you can find a local advisor through the National Association of Personal Financial Advisors (napfa.org) or the Garrett Planning Network (garrettplanningnetwork.com). Make sure that the financial advisor you select is required to work as your fiduciary, meaning that they are required to make investment decisions that are in your best interest. Make sure that there's a good personality fit between you and your advisor. Also verify that he or she has CFP, CFA or equivalent certifications. The Wall Street Journal has put together an extensive guide on how to hire a financial advisor, located at http://guides.wsj.com/personal-finance/managing-your-money/how-to-choose-a-financial-planner.

A Note for Christians About Investing

In the Bible, there are about 500 verses on prayer, fewer than 500 verses on faith and more than 2,000 verses on money and possessions. Like many other financial topics, the Bible offers several principles that Christians and Jews should be mindful of when investing their money:

- **God Provides the Ability to Produce Wealth** – "You may say to yourself, 'My power and the strength of my hands have produced this wealth for me.' But remember the Lord your God, for it is he who gives you the ability to produce wealth, and so confirms his covenant, which he swore to your ancestors, as it is today" (Deuteronomy 8:17-18).

- **Christians Should Invest in God's Kingdom** – "Sell your possessions and give to the poor. Provide purses for yourselves that will not wear out, a treasure in heaven that will never fail, where no thief comes near and no moth destroys. For where your treasure is, there your heart will be also" (Luke 12:33-34).

- **Carefully Watch Your Investments** – "Be sure you know the condition of your flocks, give careful attention to your herds; for riches do not endure forever, and a crown is not secure for all generations" (Proverbs 27:23-24).

- **Diversify Your Investments** – "Invest in seven ventures, yes, in eight; you do not know what disaster may come upon the land" (Ecclesiastes 11:2).

- **Avoid Get-Rich-Quick Schemes** – "Dishonest money dwindles away, but whoever gathers money little by little makes it grow" (Proverbs 13:11).

The most notable instruction in the Bible on investing is Jesus' parable of the talents, which is told in Matthew 25:14-30. In the story, a master entrusts his wealth to three of his servants. Each of the servants receives a sum of money in accordance with their abilities. The first servant receives five bags of gold, the second servant receives two bags of gold and the third servant receives a single bag of gold.

The master goes on a long journey and returns years later to see what the servants did with his investments. The first two servants invested their money and were able to provide good returns for their master. The third servant was afraid of losing the money and buried it in the ground.

The master scolds the servant for not even bothering to put the money on deposit with local bankers to receive interest. The master takes away his bag of gold and gives it to the first servant who was faithful with what he was given.

While the parable of the talents might seem like a straightforward lesson on using money wisely and investing it for the future, the actual meaning is much deeper. Like in Jesus' other parables, the story of the talents helps readers better understand the relationship between God and man.

In the parable of the talents, the master represents Christ and the servants represent his followers. The master's journey and return references Christ's ascension to heaven and his eventual return. The entrustment of wealth to his servants represents the various gifts and abilities that we have been given to do good with while on Earth.

The master's return and evaluation of the servants' work points to Christ's return and judgment of believers for what they did while on earth. The rewards for the faithful servants and the punishment for the unfaithful servant symbolize future spiritual rewards that faithful believers will receive in heaven.

While the parable of the talents is really an exhortation for believers to use their gifts and abilities in the service of God, we can also glean an important principle about investing from this story.

Capital that remains un-invested and "buried in the ground" doesn't do any good for anyone. If you have a large jar of change sitting in your home or money hidden in your mattress, you should probably do something more productive with it.

The parable also tells us that money that is diligently invested will grow over time. If we want to see our money multiply, we should follow the example of the two faithful servants and invest.

Using 401(k)s, Roth IRAs and Tax-Deferred Plans

One of the best ways to increase your after-tax investment returns is to invest through tax-advantaged accounts set up by the government, including 401(k) and 403(b) plans, Roth IRAs, health savings accounts (HSAs) and 529 college savings plans. If you are self-employed, you have a variety of additional choices that will allow you to set aside more money each year, such as the Simplified Employee Pension (SEP), the individual 401(k) plan and the Simple IRA.

The two most common types of retirement plans that people use are the 401(k) plan and the individual retirement arrangement (IRA). The Roth IRA is the single best retirement vehicle that investors have available to them in the U.S. As of 2016, you and your spouse can each deposit up to $5,500 per year or $6,500 per year if you are over the age of 50.

You can set up a Roth IRA through any online brokerage and can invest the money in any combination of mutual funds that you want. While you don't get an immediate tax deduction for investing in a Roth IRA, 100% of the growth and earnings generated by the investments in your Roth IRA are tax-free in retirement. You can withdraw your Roth IRA contributions tax-free at any time (although you shouldn't) and can withdraw the earnings from your Roth IRA penalty-free beginning at age 59 ½.

Technically, the income limits to invest into an IRA are $131,000 for an individual or $183,000 for families as of 2016. However, there's a loophole referred to as a "backdoor" Roth IRA that allows anyone to invest in a Roth IRA by opening a non-deductible IRA and immediately converting it to a Roth IRA. While I do most of my own investing, I have a financial advisor manage my "backdoor" Roth IRA because the steps in setting it up and moving the money around each year are a bit involved.

You may have also heard of the term traditional IRA. A traditional IRA functions very similarly to a Roth IRA, but you receive an upfront tax-deduction on your contributions and have to pay taxes on the money at retirement. In almost all cases, it's better to invest in a Roth IRA because you are investing your money after it has been taxed and before you reap the benefit of decades of compound interest. You also don't know what tax rates are going to be during retirement, so it's better to "lock in" a tax rate on your retirement dollars by investing in a Roth IRA now than taking a chance on paying significantly higher taxes in retirement.

401(k) plans are pre-tax retirement accounts that are set up through your employer. As of 2016, 401(k) plans allow employees of a company to invest $18,000 in pre-tax dollars. In many nonprofits, a 403(b) plan is offered in lieu of a 401(k) plan. Functionally, 403(b) plans are very similar to 401(k) plans and have the same contribution limits. You may receive a bonus from your employer, known as a match, when you invest in your 401(k) plan. You can begin to withdraw money from a 401(k) plan at either age 55 or 59 ½ depending on if you leave your job before age 59 ½. Some 401(k) plans also now offer a Roth option, which allow you to invest after-tax dollars and receive tax-free lifetime growth. If offered, I recommend the Roth option for the same reasons that I recommend a Roth IRA over a traditional IRA—decades of tax-free compounding growth.

If you are self-employed, you have a variety of different retirement account options that other people cannot access. If you have no employees, you can set up an individual

401(k) plan that will allow you to invest up to $53,000 of pre-tax dollars each year. There is some paperwork to set an individual 401(k) plan up, but many big brokerages have streamlined the setup process. You can also set up a simplified employee pension plan (SEP), which allows you to set aside up to 25% of your self-employment earnings each year up to $53,000 on a pre-tax basis. While individual 401(k) plans and SEP plans are the two most popular types of retirement plans for self-employed individuals, there are also SIMPLE IRAs, Money Purchase Plans (MPP) and traditional pension plans to consider as well.

After you max out your retirement plans each year, you have a couple of other tax-advantaged investing options. If you have children and want to save for their college education, you can put money away into a 529 college savings plan. The growth and income from investments inside of a 529 plan can be spent on certain education expenses tax free. If you want to open a 529 plan, read Clark Howard's 529 Plan Guide (http://clarkhoward.com/clarks-529-plan-guide), which offers specific recommendations on which state's 529 plan you should enroll in.

If you have a qualifying health insurance plan, you can also invest up to $6,750 per year (as of 2016) into a Health Savings Account (HSA). You can invest in mutual funds inside of your HSA and use the money to pay for your long-term medical expenses. When you put money into an HSA, you receive an immediate tax deduction on your contributions, but also get to spend the money tax-free on certain qualifying medical expenses. That means you can put away $6,750 per year of pre-tax money, invest it and spend it on medical expenses without ever having to pay tax on that money.

After you have maxed out your 401(k)/403(b) plan, your Roth IRA, your 529 plan (if applicable) and your HSA (if applicable), you should then just start investing in your taxable accounts. You might get pitched an annuity or a whole life insurance policy with some tax advantages, but they are usually more trouble than they are worth because of the high fees and restrictions associated with them. You also do want some money that you can live off of now in an individual account, in the event that you want to stop working before you are eligible to withdraw money from your 401(k) and Roth IRAs.

While it might seem far-fetched today that you max out all of your retirement accounts, it's entirely possible that this will become a real issue toward the end of your ten-year turnaround. If you work to increase your income and also become a super saver, you will easily max out your retirement savings options.

How to Get Market Returns

Earlier in the chapter, we learned that most mutual fund investors significantly underperform the mutual funds themselves due to switching strategies and buying and selling at inopportune times. While many investors set a laudable goal of beating the market, many investors would do much better than they are now just by getting actual market returns.

If you want to match the performance of the S&P 500, buy a low-cost S&P 500 index fund and hold onto it. It's not any more complicated than that. If you have $10,000 to invest, you can buy the Vanguard 500 Index Fund Admiral Shares (VFIAX) and pay an expense ratio of just 0.05% for the privilege of investing in the S&P 500. If you invest money into that fund or another low-cost S&P 500 fund and don't try to time the market, you will get returns that are basically equivalent to the S&P 500.

Between 1965 and 2015, the S&P 500 earned a compounded annual growth rate of 9.75% per year with dividends reinvested (http://moneychimp.com/features/market_cagr.htm). Since many investors don't average anywhere close to 10% on their money each year, you may be well served to simply invest into a low-cost S&P 500 index fund and know that you'll get about 10% per year back on your money. While you'll receive solid returns over time, the market has a lot of volatility on a month-to-month and year-to-year basis. You may have years like 2008 where the S&P 500 is down by 37% and years like 2013 where the S&P 500 is up 32.4% (see https://ycharts.com/indicators/sandp_500_total_return_annual). Because of short-term volatility, you should only invest in the market if you plan to leave the money alone for at least five years.

While investing in the S&P 500 is a good baseline for any investor, you may want to invest in other things like bonds, international stocks, commodities and real estate to diversify your money across borders and asset classes. A lot of intelligent people—including some who are much smarter than I am when it comes to investing—disagree about what the optimum asset allocation is for any given investor. The broad strokes usually tend to be that investors should hold a mix of U.S. stocks, U.S. bonds and international stocks. The percentage of your portfolio that you should have in each category will depend on your age and your risk tolerance.

Rather than suggest a specific allocation for your long-term investments, I believe it's better to point *The Ten-Year Turnaround* reader to a variety of tools and questionnaires that will help you develop an asset allocation that's best for your specific situation:

Vanguard Mutual Fund Recommendations
- https://personal.vanguard.com/us/funds/tools/recommendation

WealthFront Asset Allocation Questionnaire
- https://wealthfront.com/questions

AAII Asset Allocation Models
- http://aaii.com/asset-allocation

Betterment Asset Allocation
- https://betterment.com/portfolio

CNN Money Asset Allocation Wizard
- http://money.cnn.com/tools/assetallocwizard/assetallocwizard.html

BankRate Asset Allocation Calculator
- http://bankrate.com/calculators/retirement/asset-allocation.aspx

Should I Invest in Real Estate?

I know many people who have done very well in their lives by purchasing rental real estate. Investing in real estate can offer great diversification from the stock market and also offers excellent tax benefits.

A good rental property can easily match or even exceed the investment returns you can get in the stock market. While rental real estate can be a great investment, it's not for everyone.

Rental real estate can require much more work than owning other types of investments. In order to get started you have to save up a down payment, find a suitable property, get financing, purchase it and rent it out. You also have to collect rent each month, maintain your property, deal with emergencies and re-rent the property when a tenant moves out.

If you don't mind the extra work and can afford to purchase a property, rental real estate can be a great investment. I personally don't do much with rental real estate because I don't want to deal with the hassle and don't feel that managing rental properties is a cost-effective use of my time.

However, that doesn't mean that you shouldn't do it. Many people have built their fortunes through real estate and you can too, if that's the route that you want to go down.

Specific strategies related to real estate investment are beyond the scope of this book, primarily because I don't want to try to teach something that I have not done personally. However, there are a lot of great books and courses about rental real estate.

If I wanted to start investing in rental real estate, I would find an established landlord that owns multiple properties and has been in the business for at least ten years. I would offer to buy an hour of their time and ask them as many questions as I could about the industry. I would also read several books about rental real estate and complete a reputable course or seminar about investing in rental real estate.

Dividend Growth: The Investment Strategy That Beats the S&P 500

At the beginning of this chapter, I promised that I would show you an investment strategy that has historically outperformed the S&P 500 with less volatility. If you know anything about the investment world, that's an awfully big claim. Because most money managers can't consistently outperform their benchmarks, it would be surprising to anyone to find a strategy that has outperformed the market over a long period of time. While there's no way to be sure that the investment strategy that I use will continue to outperform the market in the future, it has done far better than the S&P 500 since at least the early 90's.

No, I haven't stumbled across a little-known investment strategy that the market missed. This strategy isn't complicated or exotic and is a lot more boring than you might think.

I invest in a series of individual stocks that pay strong dividends and have a history of raising their dividends over time. Previously, I had been a staunch proponent of investing in index funds, but I became a believer in dividend-paying stocks after seeing how well they perform through many different types of markets.

The S&P 500 publishes a list of companies that have raised their dividends every year for at least 25 years in a row. The Indexology blog recently published a chart comparing the performance of the S&P Dividend Aristocrats Index compared to the S&P 500. While investing in the S&P 500 resulted in cumulative returns of about 1,100% during this time frame, the S&P 500 Dividend Aristocrats Index had cumulative returns of more than 1,900%.

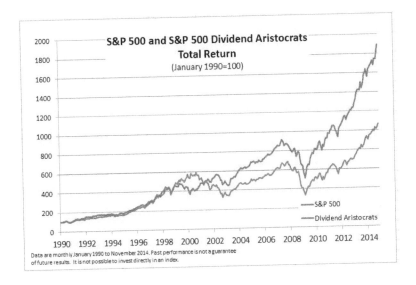

S&P 500 and S&P 500 Dividend Aristocrats Total Return
(January 1990=100)

Data are monthly January 1990 to November 2014. Past performance is not a guarantee of future results. It is not possible to invest directly in an index.

Why does investing in dividend stocks work so well? The magic isn't in the dividends themselves, but in the companies that consistently pay strong dividends. If a company is going to pay out a good chunk of their earnings in the form of a dividend, they are going to have to have the cash flow to support that dividend. Because they have to pay out a dividend each quarter and the market will expect them to raise their dividend by 5-10% each year, they will need to have consistently strong earnings and steadily grow their earnings over time. If a company raises their dividend for 25 consecutive years, there is a pretty strong chance that they have solid earnings, cash flow and growth potential, which makes them great companies to invest in regardless of whether or not they paid a dividend.

The companies in the S&P 500 Dividend Aristocrats index tend to be well-established blue chip companies, like McDonald's, Target, Procter & Gamble, Chevron, Coca-Cola, Verizon and Johnson & Johnson. These are large established players and they tend to be less volatile than the broader market. The S&P 500 Dividend Aristocrats index has a beta that averages around 0.9, which means that those companies are, on average, 10% less volatile than the broader market. My personal portfolio, which consists almost entirely of established dividend payers, has a beta of just 0.66, meaning that I can avoid as much as a third of the wild price swings of the market.

Impressive returns and lower volatility aren't the only benefits of investing in established dividend-paying stocks. Dividend investing has the added benefit of being a form of income investing.

Whenever you are ready to start living off of your investments, you can simply stop automatically reinvesting your dividends and start living off the dividend payments that you receive each month. You'll receive a steady stream of cash flow without having to sell a single share of the companies that you own. You know that the payments you're receiving are relatively secure and will likely go up by 5%-10% each year if you invest in solid dividend-paying companies.

If you want to put together a portfolio of dividend growth stocks, you should look for companies that have raised their dividend every year for at least ten years. When a company has a track record of raising their dividend over a long period of time, you know that the company is committed to its dividend and will likely continue to raise its dividend in the future. Because this strategy is focused on generating long-term income that you can live off, you should also focus on stocks that have a dividend yield of at least 3.5%. It's a lot easier to create a retirement account when your average portfolio yield is in the 4-5% range than it is with 1-3% dividends more common to the S&P 500.

When selecting dividend growth stocks to invest in, you also want to make sure that the company will have the cash flow to continue to support its dividend. You can verify a company's ability to keep paying its dividend by looking at its dividend payout ratio, which is simply the percentage of earnings the company pays out as a dividend. Ideally, a company should be paying out no more than 75% of its earnings in dividends. REITs are the exception to this rule, as they are required to pay out 90% of their earnings as distributions to their shareholders. If a company is committed to paying out more in dividends than it earns each quarter, you know that company has a major risk of cutting its dividend. If you invest in companies that have payout ratios around 50%, you can be reasonably sure your dividend is safe and that the company has plenty of room to raise their dividend over time.

If you would like to explore dividend growth investing, I highly recommend that you read *The Ultimate Dividend Playbook* by Josh Peters, who is the director of equity income strategy for Morningstar, and *Get Rich with Dividends* by Marc Lichtenfeld. These two books lay out how to create a portfolio of dividend growth stocks in great detail. Peters also publishes a monthly newsletter called "Morningstar Dividend Investor" (http://mdi.morningstar.com), which offers an excellent dividend growth model portfolio that any investor can easily replicate.

It would be nice to be able to recommend a mutual fund or an ETF that selects dividend growth stocks that meet the criteria mentioned above, but one doesn't exist. While there are a number of dividend growth mutual funds and ETFs, most of them have a lower average yield than we are looking for. They also generally don't factor in a company's payout ratio and include stocks that have dividend yields in the 1-3% range. If you want to build a portfolio of dividend growth stocks, the best way to do it is to build an investment portfolio of 10 to 25 companies that meet the criteria specified above. While this might sound like a daunting task, model portfolios such as the one published by "Morningstar Dividend Investor" can serve as a great starting point to identify companies you might want to put in your portfolio.

For my personal investment strategy, I currently own a collection of 27 different dividend stocks in my taxable account. The portfolio has an average dividend yield of 4.4%, an average payout of 79% and an average annual dividend growth rate of 7.9% over the last three years. I've chosen not to include a list of stocks in my portfolio in this book, because they can and do change over time. If you really want to know what stocks I personally own, you can find an up-to-date list of my holdings in the terms of service page on MarketBeat.com under the "investment ownership disclaimer" section. I currently only use the dividend growth strategy in my taxable account. In my Roth IRA and my Individual 401(k) accounts, I use a more traditional mix of index funds, because the dividend growth strategy is hard to replicate without owning individual stocks.

Wrap-up

We have covered a lot of important ground in this chapter. We examined common investing mistakes, whether or not to use a financial advisor, various types of retirement accounts, asset allocation, and dividend growth investing. While there's a lot of technical know-how that goes into investing, it's important to keep the big picture in mind. Remember that we are trying to build a stream of investment income that will eventually eliminate the need to earn a salary from a job. By investing a good chunk of your income into broadly diversified investments each month, you will build a sizable investment portfolio over time that will generate an income stream you can live off when you reach financial freedom.

Action Steps

❏ Learn the four major investment traps so that you can avoid them.

❏ Decide if you want to hire a financial advisor to manage your money.

❏ Set up your retirement savings accounts if you haven't already.

❏ Determine what asset allocation you want to use for your investments.

❏ Set up an automatic savings plan so that you are automatically investing money each month.

Chapter Eight:
Insurance, Taxes and Other Boring Financial Topics

While much of this book has been devoted to playing offense in the game of wealth building by increasing your income and investing for the future, we also need to play defense. It won't do you any good to make a bunch of money if you aren't able to keep any of it due to a liability claim, a lawsuit settlement or a big tax bill.

If you want to keep the wealth you are working hard to build, you have to learn about the tax code and take a variety of steps to legally reduce your tax burden. You also need to carry the appropriate types of insurance so that you don't get hit with a big liability claim if you are in a car accident or someone breaks their leg on your sidewalk. Finally, you need to arrange your life in such a way that you won't become the target of frivolous lawsuits from people who want a piece of your wealth.

Insurance

Some people see paying insurance premiums as a waste of money. If you don't have a claim during the term of your policy, you don't get anything for your money. If you never have an insurance claim, that's entirely true. However, you don't buy insurance to cover what you know is going to happen. You buy it to cover things that you can't possibly predict.

In 2012, my son Micah was born 10 weeks before his expected due date. He weighed 3 pounds, 1 ounce, and had to spend the first 71 days of his life in a neonatal intensive care unit. Prior to his premature birth, we had a smooth pregnancy and had no idea that anything was wrong. If we hadn't had insurance, we would have paid more than $700,000 in medical bills for the care that Micah received in the first year of his life. Because we had a good health insurance policy in place, our total out-of-pocket costs were around $15,000 when all was said and done. It was still a big bill to pay, but nothing compared to what it could have been without insurance.

It's important to have a series of insurance policies in place to cover "black swan" events that you normally would never expect to happen and won't possibly be able to pay for without insurance. If you are in a major auto accident, if you become disabled, or if your house burns down, you don't want to be the one footing the bill. It's much better to pay a manageable annual fee to cover the risks associated with these things than it is to get hit with a large bill that you can't possibly pay down the line.

There are several types of insurance policies that you should probably own in order to be prepared:

- **Homeowner's or Renter's Insurance** – These policies will cover your material possessions in the event that something happens to your home or the apartment that you live in. Always buy replacement-cost insurance, which will require the insurance company to pay you enough to replace your possessions and not just compensate you for the value that the insurance company decides your stuff is worth. If you are a homeowner, over insure the value of your home because it often costs more to repair a home severely damaged by fire or other disasters than it does to build a new home from the ground up. If you live in a flood zone, you should also carry a separate flood insurance policy because homeowner's insurance policies typically do not cover damage by flood.

- **Car Insurance** – Every state requires that automobile owners carry liability insurance, but the minimum amount of insurance required by states is often not enough to pay for the vehicle damage and medical bills that can result from a major accident. Most insurance experts recommend buying at least a "100/300" policy, which covers $100,000 in medical expenses per person involved and $300,000 total for all of the individuals involved in an accident. If you have a net worth of more than $300,000, buy the maximum available liability coverage (typically $500,000 per accident) so that your assets are protected in the event of a lawsuit stemming from an automobile accident.

- **Life Insurance** – If you have a spouse or children, purchase a 20-year or 30-year level term life insurance policy to provide for your family in the event of your death. Purchase at least ten times your annual income in coverage so that your loved ones can invest the money and live off of the income. Avoid whole life, universal life, and variable life policies because of the high cost and fees associated with these types of policies.

- **Health Insurance** – Medical expenses are responsible for 62% of all bankruptcies in the United States (http://investopedia.com/financial-edge/0310/top-5-reasons-people-go-bankrupt.aspx). Because of the incredibly high cost of medical care in the United States, everyone should get a health insurance policy through their employer, through one of the state insurance exchanges or through an independent insurance agent. If you are unable to pay for health insurance, see if you qualify for a subsidy under the Affordable Care Act. You might also consider faith-based health insurance alternatives, such as Christian Healthcare Ministries (chministries.org), Samaritan Ministries (samaritanministries.org), Medi-Share (mychristiancare.org) or Liberty HealthShare (libertyhealthshare.org).

- **Long-Term Disability Insurance** – You are four times more likely to be permanently disabled than you are to die by the age of 65 (http://affordableinsuranceprotection.com/death_vs_

disability). A typical 35-year old adult has a 21-24% risk of becoming disabled for three months or longer during their working years (http://disabilitycanhappen.org/chances_disability/disability_stats.asp). Buy a policy that will cover at least 65% of your income if you become disabled. Make sure to pay for long-term disability with after-tax money so that the benefits you receive will be tax free. Also, try to get a policy that covers you if you are unable to continue working in your occupation at the time of the extended illness or accident. The cheapest way to buy long-term disability insurance is through an employer, but an independent insurance agent can help you buy a policy if employer-offered long-term disability insurance isn't an option for you.

- **Long-Term Care Insurance** – After the age of 65, 70% of people will have a nursing home stay or need some other form of long-term care (http://longtermcare.gov/the-basics/how-much-care-will-you-need) during their lives. Since the cost of nursing home care averages more than $6,000 per month, it's important to cover the risk of needing to stay in a managed care facility by buying long-term care insurance. According to the American Association of Long-Term Care Insurance, the best time to purchase long-term care coverage is in your mid 50s (http://aaltci.org/long-term-care-insurance/learning-center/best-age-to-buy-long-term-care-insurance.php). If you purchase a policy before your mid 50s, you are probably wasting money because the possibility that you will need long-term care is pretty low. If you wait until your 60s to purchase long-term care insurance, the cost of the policy will rise dramatically.

- **Umbrella Liability Insurance** – If you have a high net worth, purchase an umbrella liability policy that will protect you from major claims and lawsuits. An umbrella policy will provide additional liability coverage above the limits of your homeowner's and auto insurance policies. For example, your auto insurance might cover the first $500,000 of total liability. Your umbrella policy might add $1 or $2 million of extra liability coverage after your auto insurance liability caps out. Umbrella policies may also cover you from types of liability that your other policies don't cover, such as false arrest, libel, slander, malicious prosecution, and mental anguish. Umbrella insurance is very affordable and can be purchased from every major insurance company.

The seven types of insurance listed above are must-haves in most situations, but there are also many other types of insurance that you just don't need. Never buy an insurance policy or an extended warranty for anything that you can easily cover with an emergency fund. That means you shouldn't ever buy an extended warranty on things like TVs, computers and appliances. Never buy an insurance policy when there is no insurable need.

For example, children do not need life insurance because no one depends on their income to live. There are also many types of duplicative insurance policies that replicate what your existing insurance policies already cover, such as cancer insurance, accidental death insurance, hospital insurance and mortgage protection insurance. These things are already covered by your health insurance and life insurance and do not need to be double insured.

While it's incredibly easy to shop for insurance online these days, I think it's best to work with an independent insurance agent who can shop for policies among many different insurers on your behalf. A good independent agent will be able to educate you on exactly what policies you need, what features you need in each policy and what coverage levels to get for each type of policy.

Working with an independent agent will also give you an ally in the event that you have to file a claim or have a dispute with an insurance company. The best way to find an independent insurance agent is to ask for recommendations from friends and family members. If no one has a recommendation, it's very easy to find a local independent agent through Google or the local Yellow Pages.

My Insurance Action Plan

Which of the seven key types of insurance are you missing? What policies do you have that you haven't reviewed in a while? Do you need to change your coverage limits on any of your policies? Do you have any gimmick policies that you need to cancel?

Write down what action steps you need to take in order to get the appropriate policies with the appropriate level of coverage in place.

_____

_____

_____

_____

_____

_____

_____

_____

_____

_____

_____

_____

_____

Taxes

Taxes are a reality of life in every country in the world. Whether you agree with your country's tax system or not, you have to pay whatever the tax code says is your fair share. If you plan on becoming wealthy, you should expect that your fair share of the nation's tax bill will be larger than everyone else's fair share. 45.3% of American families pay no federal income tax (http://cnbc.com/2015/10/09/775-million-households-are-not-paying-federal-income-taxes.html) and the top 10% of income earners pay 68% of all federal income taxes (http://heritage.org/federalbudget/top10-percent-income-earners). Most countries place a disproportionately large tax burden on the wealthy and the United States is no exception.

I personally paid more than $650,000 in taxes in 2015 and spent five times more on my tax bill than on all of my other living expenses combined. If you plan on becoming wealthy during your ten-year turnaround, learn to use the tax code to your advantage and limit your federal tax liability each year.

You should never evade paying taxes by filing a fraudulent return or not filing a return at all, but you should do whatever you can within the bounds of the tax code to minimize your tax burden.

The government rewards certain activities and punishes other activities through the tax code. If the government wants more of something, they set up a tax deduction, tax credit or other special tax program to reward that activity. For example, the government wants people to go to college, so they have set up a variety of credits and deductions that make attending college more affordable. The government also wants people to have children, so tax filers receive a credit each year for every child that they have. Conversely, the government taxes activities that it wants less of. This is why the federal government charges an excise tax on the sale of tobacco and alcohol. In order to minimize your tax burden, you need to do more of the activities that the government wants you to do and do fewer of the activities that the government doesn't want you to do.

Here are some activities that the government rewards in the tax system:

- **Running a Business** – Business owners can receive a variety of tax benefits that others can't receive, such as the home office deduction, the mileage deduction, the self-employed health insurance deduction, and business expense deductions. Business owners also are able to put away more in specialized retirement plans, individual 401(k)s, and SEPs. This doesn't mean that business owners get off easy though. Most self-employed people have to pay self-employment tax to cover the employer's side of Social Security and Medicare. Not to mention, many business owners are in the higher tax brackets because they often have higher incomes.

- **Saving for Retirement** – By investing money into a Roth IRA, your company's 401(k) plan, or another type of retirement plan, you can save money for retirement on a tax-deferred or tax-free basis depending on what type of account you are investing in.

- **Giving to Charity** – You can receive a tax deduction for 100% of the charitable gifts that you make to any 501(c)(3) nonprofit organization. This includes any gifts that you make to your local church and any other charitable organization that you might give to.

- **Buying a Home** – You can receive a tax deduction for your mortgage interest and for property taxes that you pay. The mortgage interest deduction is often one of the biggest tax deductions on many people's tax return. When you go to sell your home, the first $250,000 (if you're single) or $500,000 (if you're married) of capital gains are excluded from your taxes. Even if your house has substantially risen in price, you still probably won't have to pay any taxes on it.

- **Investing in Rental Real Estate** – Landlords receive a tax deduction for the depreciation of the value of the property that they buy, which often offsets any income tax liability created by rental income. Landlords can also deduct any expenses related to the maintenance of their home. There are some specific rules about what you can deduct immediately and what needs to be depreciated over several years, so do additional research or talk to your tax professional before claiming these deductions.

- **Having Children** – You can receive a tax credit of $1,000 per child as of the 2015 tax year. Each additional child also adds a dependent to your tax return, which will further reduce your tax burden.

- **Paying State Taxes** – You can receive a deduction on your federal taxes for any state taxes that you pay, including sales tax, property tax, and income tax.

- **Going to College** – There are a variety of different tax credits and deductions available for people going to college and the parents of people going to college. If you are in college or have children going to college, research the American opportunity credit, the life-long learning credit, the tuition and fees deduction, and the student loan interest deduction. There are also specialized investment accounts including the 529 college savings plan and the Coverdell education savings account that allow people to put money away for college on a tax-advantaged basis.

- **Investing in Stocks and Municipal Bonds** – Because the government wants to encourage investment, capital gains and dividends are taxed at a lower tax rate than other types of income. Income from investing in municipal bonds is totally tax-free.

- **Finding a Job** – You can receive a deduction for any expenses related to a job search, with some limitations. If you are moving to another city for a new job, you can also deduct your moving expenses from your taxes.

- **Buying Health Insurance** – The government allows employers to furnish their employees with health insurance without creating an income tax liability for the employee. If you are self-employed, you can deduct the cost of health insurance from your tax return.

- **Going Green** – There are a variety of federal tax credits available that will reduce the cost of adding energy efficient features to your home, such as insulation, roofing, water heaters and new windows. Details can be found on the EnergyStar website (https://energystar.gov/about/federal_tax_credits).

- **Paying for Medical Expenses** – You can deduct qualified medical expenses that are more than 10% of your adjusted gross income each year. If you make $50,000 and have $10,000 in medical expenses, you will be able to deduct $5,000 from your taxes.

The list of activities that the government encourages above is designed to give you the flavor of the types of things that can reduce your taxes. Remember that every deduction, credit and exclusion has a specific set of criteria that you must meet to claim the credit. Additionally, tax law changes every year. If you are reading this book five years after it was first published, some of the deductions and credits listed above have probably changed. Don't take a deduction or a credit on your next tax return solely based on the information in this chapter. Consult a tax professional or do your own research before taking any of these deductions.

Deductions and credits are the primary way that you'll be able to reduce your tax burden, but those aren't the only things that you can do to reduce your taxes. Here are some additional tips related to taxes that might help reduce your overall tax burden:

- **Hire a Professional** – The tax code is incredibly complex and is too difficult for someone who doesn't specialize in taxes to understand. If you have a very basic return and make less than $50,000 per year, go ahead and use TurboTax. If you're an entrepreneur, make more than $50,000 per year or otherwise have a complicated return, have a tax professional do your taxes. A good tax person can often find deductions and credits that you missed and make far fewer mistakes than you would doing your own taxes. Also, if the IRS has a question about your return or audits your taxes, your tax person will be the one who has to deal with them.

- **Review a Deduction Checklist** – There are a variety of tools, checklists and questionnaires online that will help you find deductions and credits that you might otherwise have missed. A good place to start is to do a web search for keywords like "tax deduction checklist" and "commonly missed tax deductions," which will yield dozens of different lists that you can check to make sure that you didn't miss out on any deductions, credits or exclusions.

- **Move to a Low Tax State** – Your tax burden will vary dramatically based on which state you live in. In New York, there's a 4.0-8.875% sales tax depending on what municipality you're in, a minimum state income tax of 6.65%, a state capital gains tax of 8.8%, a corporate income tax of 7.1% and an average statewide property tax of 1.5% (https://smartasset.com/taxes/new-york-property-tax-calculator). Compare this to states like South Dakota that have a 4.5-6.5% sales tax depending on what city you're in, no state income tax, no corporate income tax, no capital gains tax and an average property tax rate of 1.36%. If you make a high income, consider moving across a state line if it means you will benefit from a dramatically lower tax burden.

- **Delay Income and Accelerate Expenses** – If it's near the end of the year, consider speeding up any tax deductible expenses you plan on making before the year is out. If you're an entrepreneur and have money coming in, maybe wait until after the first of the year to send out invoices. While this won't eliminate your tax burden, it will mean that you won't have to pay taxes on the income you push forward for over a year.

- **Don't Try to Get a Tax Refund** – If you receive a large tax refund each year because you overpaid in taxes, adjust your withholding so that you aren't giving the government an interest-free loan every year. You are better off putting that money immediately to work helping you reach your financial goals than letting the government hold onto it until you file your tax return.

While it's impossible to completely avoid paying taxes without breaking the law, there are lots of actionable steps that you can take to reduce your total tax burden. By doing the things that the government rewards in the tax system and by following some of the other recommendations above, you should be able to find significant tax savings each year.

A Note to Christians About Paying Taxes

The Bible plainly states that Christians should submit to governing authorities and pay the taxes imposed on them. In Matthew's Gospel, a group of Pharisees challenged Jesus and asked him whether or not it was right to pay taxes to Rome (Matthew 22:16-22). Jesus wisely responded that they should "give back to Caesar what is Caesar's; and give to God what is God's." In his response, Jesus acknowledged that the government makes lawful requests of its citizens and that we must be obedient to the government in political and civil matters.

The Apostle Paul elaborates on this matter in the book of Romans:

> *Let everyone be subject to the governing authorities, for there is no authority except that which God has established. The authorities that exist have been established by God. Consequently, whoever rebels against the authority is rebelling against what God has instituted, and those who do so will bring judgment on themselves. For rulers hold no terror for those who do right, but for those who do wrong. Do you want to be free from fear of the one in authority? Then do what is right and you will be commended. For the one in authority is God's servant for your good. But if you do wrong, be afraid, for rulers do not bear the sword for no reason. They are God's servants, agents of wrath to bring punishment on the wrongdoer. Therefore, it is necessary to submit to the authorities, not only because of possible punishment but also as a matter of conscience. This is also why you pay taxes, for the authorities are God's servants, who give their full time to governing. Give to everyone what you owe them: If you owe taxes, pay taxes; if revenue, then revenue; if respect, then respect; if honor, then honor. (Romans 13:1-7)*

Some Christians may argue that they should avoid paying taxes because the government does things that are sinful or otherwise un-Christian. Those familiar with the practices of the Roman government during the time Jesus was alive immediately recognize that this isn't a valid excuse for Christians not to pay taxes.

Tiberius Caesar, who was the emperor of Rome from 14 to 37 A.D., summarily executed his political opponents without trial, appointed corrupt governors and had a reputation for severe sexual perversion. His line of successors, including Caligula, Claudius and Nero, weren't any better. Claudius thought he should be deified as emperor and Nero extensively persecuted Christians for their beliefs. Despite the many wrongdoings of the Roman emperors, which far exceed any wrongs currently happening in any developed country in the world, both Jesus and Paul told Christians to pay their taxes to Rome.

Protecting Yourself from Lawsuits

Have you heard of the lawsuit where a family living off welfare was sued for $7 million? No, of course you haven't. Lawsuits generally don't get filed against people with few assets because you can't squeeze blood from a turnip.

Personal liability and injury cases get filed against wealthy people, because that's where the money is. If you are on the path to becoming wealthy, you have an increased risk of being targeted for a personal liability lawsuit. You never know when you will get in an accident with someone or when someone will be injured on your property and decide that they need a piece of your money.

I'm not a lawyer and can't offer actual legal advice, so consult with a good attorney before taking any steps that I recommend to reduce the likelihood of getting sued. Here are some general tips to protect yourself from lawsuits as you begin to build wealth:

- **Increase Your Liability Insurance** – Umbrella liability insurance is your first defense against a potential liability lawsuit. You should have at least enough liability insurance to cover your personal net worth. For instance, if you are worth $3 million between your home, your investments and your business interests, you should have at least $3 million in liability coverage. At $200-$300 per year for each $1 million of coverage, having a good umbrella liability is the cheapest way to defend yourself from lawsuits.

- **Avoid Showing Off Lavish Wealth** – If no one knows that you have a high net worth, you won't have a target on your back for lawsuits. For this and many other reasons, I recommend against lavish displays of wealth such as high-end luxury vehicles and million-dollar homes that will tip everyone off to the fact that you have a pile of money they can go after.

- **Put Businesses and Rental Properties in a Limited Liability Company (LLC)** – If you have a rental property or own a business, consider putting it in a LLC. That way, if someone sues your business, they can only go after the assets inside of the limited liability company rather than any assets that you own personally.

- **Put Business Partnerships on Paper** – You may be at risk for the actions of any of your potential business partners. If you and your partner operate as a general partnership and your partner gets sued, your personal assets could be at risk because of the lawsuit. Put general partnerships inside of an LLC to provide yourself with legal protection.

- **Nip Potential Issues in the Bud** – If someone feels personally wronged by you, take action to rectify the situation before it escalates into a lawsuit. Even if you feel that you are in the right, a simple apology can stop many issues before they escalate. People get angry, hateful and litigious when they stop seeing someone as a human being and only see that person as a source of wrongdoing. A simple apology can often catch someone flat-footed and cause them to remember that they are dealing with another human. Of course, a good lawyer will tell you to not admit any wrongdoing when there's a risk of a lawsuit, so be careful what you say and what you do to try to rectify any potentially litigious situation.

- **Get Help from a Lawyer** – If you have a personal net worth of more than $1 or $2 million, it's worth sitting down with an asset protection lawyer and asking them what specific steps you can take to mitigate the risk of a lawsuit and protect your assets in the event you are sued. A good lawyer can also go over advanced strategies beyond the scope of this book, like setting up trusts. While you might spend several hundred dollars on a consultation, it's an incredibly affordable insurance policy to have if you do get sued.

I have personally been sued once in my life over a business dispute with a former employer. While I won't go into detail about the suit, there was a difference of opinion as to what my legal obligations were to them. I thought I was right. They thought I was wrong. While I do believe I would have ultimately prevailed in the lawsuit, I opted for a quick settlement that cost me a meaningful (but not outrageous) amount of money.

Another business owner in Sioux Falls once told me that if you can settle any lawsuit for less than $20,000, you probably should. Defending a lawsuit can be an incredibly expensive and time consuming exercise that can cost $30,000-$50,000 and take more than a year of your life. If you get sued and there's a possibility of a quick, reasonable, and affordable settlement, consider taking it even if you do think you would ultimately win the suit. There's real value in getting past a lawsuit so that you can go on with life, even if it costs you some money up front.

Wrap-up

Playing defense is an important aspect to any wealth building effort. Increasing your income and investing your money will allow you to build wealth. Reducing your tax burden and mitigating the risk of a lawsuit or major insurance event will prevent you from losing your wealth. Many of the worst-case scenarios listed in this chapter may never happen to you. It's not very likely that your house will burn down, that you will get sued, that you will be audited by the IRS or that you will get into a major car accident. But while the risk of these events happening in your life is pretty low, they do happen to some people. It's better to be prepared for an event that may never happen to you than to take a major financial hit that you could have easily prevented. By buying the right insurance policies and taking steps to minimize the risk of a lawsuit, you can substantially mitigate the risk of facing a catastrophic financial event in your life.

Action Steps

- ☐ Review your insurance policies and make sure that you carry the types of coverage recommended in this chapter.

- ☐ Look for tax deductions and credits you may have missed to reduce your tax bill.

- ☐ Take any appropriate steps to reduce the likelihood of being sued.

Chapter Nine:
The Joy of Charitable Giving

Only a life lived for others is a life worthwhile.
— Albert Einstein

There are only so many different things that you can do with money. You can spend it on yourself, you can save and invest it for the future or you can give it away.

As I have built wealth, I have realized that owning a lot of nice stuff doesn't really make anyone that much happier. Sure, it's fun to buy a new car, move into a nicer house and get the latest hot new gadget, but that happiness doesn't last. A few weeks after a major purchase, the new thing that you just bought becomes a regular part of your life. You aren't any happier than you were before, and now you have one more possession to take care of.

Seeing your net worth go up each month also loses its luster after a while. Once you have all of your needs taken care of, any additional money that you make or earn from your investments starts to feel like monopoly money. Yes, the number in your brokerage account is going up every month, but it's not changing your lifestyle in any meaningful way. You can continue to set money aside for "the future," but your wealth doesn't do anyone any good if you won't ever need the money. Having a high net worth isn't nearly as important as the process by which you build your wealth. In other words, the journey is more important than the destination. If you become a person capable of building wealth, it doesn't really matter how much money is actually in your bank accounts because you can always go out and build more wealth.

What has created joy and happiness in my life is engaging in unique experiences through travel and giving money to worthy causes. Jesus said that it is better to give than to receive, and this has definitely been true in my life.

While it's hard to communicate the joy that a person can feel by doing good in the world with their money, giving to worthy causes has created far more pleasure and happiness in my life than owning a nicer car or a bigger home ever would. It's incredibly rewarding to see other people's lives fundamentally changed for the better because of your giving.

Imagine how you could change someone's life forever by building a school in Africa, supporting a nonprofit that rescues women from the sex trade, or funding a homeless shelter.

How to Discover the Joy of Giving

If you haven't done much charitable giving in your life and have yet to discover the joy of giving, the best thing that you can do is find a cause that you are incredibly passionate about and watch your money do good work. For your first few gifts, I suggest giving to smaller organizations or a specific project at larger organizations so that you can see the tangible impact that your actual dollars have on an organization. If at all possible, volunteer some of your time at the organization so that you can meet the people who are affected by the organization you are giving to. You might also consider finding a needy family and helping them directly so that you can see the immediate results your dollars bring about in their life. The goal is to give to a cause that's both close to your heart and one where the effects of your money are quickly and visibly manifest. Watching the power of your charitable giving in action is the best way to discover the personal happiness that providing joy to others can bring.

While some people give to charity to get recognition and to be seen as a generous person, I think this is the wrong motivation for giving. The joy that you receive from giving should come from seeing your money do good in the world, not because you receive kudos from those around you for being a generous person. If you are only giving to charity because you want to receive recognition for your gifts, you're missing the point. Giving should never be about what the giver can get out of making a gift. Giving is an act of humility, an acknowledgement that we are part of a larger world that doesn't center around us and a recognition that we have a responsibility to take care of the larger world and the people in it.

How Much Money Should I Give to Charity?

Depending on what survey you read, the average American family gives between 2% and 3% of their annual income to charity each year. In 2014, individuals gave a total of $258.5 billion to charity in the United States. Corporations accounted for $17.7 billion in giving and foundations accounted for $53.7 billion in giving in the same year (http://nptrust.org/philanthropic-resources/charitable-giving-statistics). The average dollar amount of charitable gifts per family is $2,974 per year.

As individuals on the pathway to financial freedom, should we shoot for the average and try to give 3% of income to charity each year? Should we do less giving because we are trying to save money for the future, or should we give much more than 3% of our income, based on our ability to produce income and do good in the world?

Given that 1.3 billion people in the world live in extreme poverty and 2.5 billion people live on less than $2.50 per day (https://dosomething.org/us/facts/11-facts-about-global-poverty), I can't personally feel good about giving an average percentage of my income to charity. There are simply too many outstanding needs for those of us who plan to be very successful to merely give an average amount of our income to charity. I believe that the most capable, most ambitious and most successful people in the world need to give more of their time and money than the average if we are going to tackle the world's problems.

Many major world religions—including Judaism, Christianity, Sikhism, and in some cases Islam—suggest that people give 10% of their income to charity. This is based on the ancient Mosaic principle of giving a tenth of one's income, known as a tithe, to God (Leviticus 27:31-33).

While religious organizations no longer have a monopoly on charitable works in the world, 10% of one's income seems to be a very good baseline target amount of money to give to charity. If Americans were to increase their annual giving from 3% to 10% of their incomes, there would be an additional $600 billion per year available for charitable organizations to do good in the world.

Jeffrey Sachs, author of *The End of Poverty*, estimates that it would cost $175 billion per year to eliminate extreme poverty in the world over the next 20 years. If everyone were to give 10%, we could eliminate extreme poverty and still have $425 billion left over to fight disease, solve social problems and fund religious activities.

If you aren't giving any of your income to charity right now or are only giving an average percentage of your income, I suggest slowly working your way up to 10% or even beyond that. If you are giving 2% of your income this year, shoot for 3 or 4% next year and 5 or 6% the year after that. You don't have to jump to giving 10% of your income right away and your long-term giving target doesn't even have to be exactly 10%, but I believe that is the general target you should aim for.

Won't Giving Slow Down My Wealth-Building Process?

If your primary financial goal is achieving financial freedom by building an investment portfolio that can pay for your living expenses, you might be tempted not to give while you build wealth, so that you can achieve financial freedom faster. If you give $5,000 to charity each year, that's $5,000 that won't go into your retirement accounts. From a purely mathematical perspective, being generous comes at the expense of faster wealth building. However, when considering this trade-off, you may be making the assumption that you will have the same income, opportunities and success regardless of how much you give to charity. But if new career or business opportunities come along and you make more money because you are known as a generous person, the math isn't as clear-cut as a basic spreadsheet might indicate.

In the business world, there are people with an abundance mindset and others with a scarcity mindset. Those with an abundance mindset believe that there's plenty of opportunity and success available to everyone and are more than happy to help others with their time and money. People with a scarcity mindset believe that there is only so much success and wealth to go around and that they need to grab as much of it as possible and hold onto it tightly. People with a scarcity mindset regularly take and ask from other people, exhibit greed and rarely give back to anyone else.

It's very easy to identify whether someone is operating out of a mindset of abundance or scarcity, and the best business and career opportunities present themselves to people with an abundance mindset. By being generous with your time and money, you will naturally build a form of political capital with the community around you. You will build connections that you wouldn't otherwise have. This capital will enable you to ask people for favors. People will think of you positively and more opportunities will show up at your door because you are well-respected and appreciated in your community.

Conversely, most people are pretty good at sniffing out greed and selfishness. If you never help others and are only concerned about how you can help yourself, people will recognize that and keep their distance.

Personally, I have never thought of charitable giving as something that hinders or slows down wealth building. While you may be saving slightly less money in the short term because you are giving some of it to charity, this result is far outweighed by the opportunities that arise as a result of operating in a mindset of abundance.

Of course, there's not a 1-1 correlation between how much money you give and the success that comes back to you. However, I can attest to the fact that I wouldn't have nearly the success that I have today if I hadn't been generous and helpful to others along the way. And even if charitable giving did slow down my wealth building, I frankly don't care, because charitable giving is more important to me than growing my net worth faster.

Who Should I Give To?

There are currently more than 1.5 million charitable organizations, more than 315,000 religious congregations and more than 86,000 foundations in the United States (http://nptrust.org/philanthropic-resources/charitable-giving-statistics). Given the wide variety of philanthropic organizations out there, it can be hard to choose which organizations are most deserving of your money. While the nonprofit organizations you land on will invariably be different from the ones that I have selected, I believe there are some basic criteria which anyone can use to evaluate whether or not he or she should give to an organization:

- **Give Toward Your Passion** – Select organizations whose missions you are genuinely passionate about. My firstborn son, Micah, was born 10 weeks early. That experience gave our family a unique appreciation for medical care and research relating to premature babies. Because of our passion in this area, my wife and I support our state chapter of the March of Dimes (marchofdimes.org). Don't make a gift just because a fundraiser asks you for money; make a gift to an organization because you care deeply about its mission.

- **Give Through Relationships** – Favor organizations with which you have personal contact over organizations that you have no personal affiliation with. When you know someone at an organization, you can more easily get updates as to what the organization is doing and be aware of opportunities to serve with your time in addition to your money.

- **Verify Use of Donor Dollars** – Let's face it. Some nonprofits are run better than others. Some nonprofits are beacons of efficiency and the vast majority of the money they receive goes toward their mission. Other organizations don't spend money well or spend a large portion of the money they receive on additional fundraising and administrative expenses. As I write this book, the Wounded Warrior Project was recently called out for having overhead expenses that amounted to 40% of its received donations (http://washingtontimes.com/news/2016/jan/27/wounded-warrior-project-accused-of-wasting-donor-m). I imagine most of their donors were shocked to learn that only 60% of their gifts were going to help veterans. Use websites like Charity Watch (charitywatch.org), Charity Navigator (charitynavigator.org) and the Evangelical Financial Accountability

Association (efca.org) to determine how much of an organization's money is actually going toward their mission. You can also look up financial reports for nonprofits on Guidestar (guidestar.org) and look up ratings for charities on the Better Business Bureau website (http://give.org/reports/index.asp).

- **Don't Make Small Token Gifts** – If someone from a large national charity that you aren't interested in asks you for money, you might be tempted to give a token gift of $10 or $25 to appease them. Given that many large charities pelt their donors with direct mail, the organization may be better off not receiving a gift from you at all. If you make a single token gift and the organization spends more money than you gave trying to get you to make additional gifts through direct mail, you haven't done anyone any good with your gift.

- **Don't Give Out of Obligation** – I don't recommend making gifts just because a fundraiser asks you for money or because you feel obligated to give to a specific charity. You may end up resenting the fundraiser that asked you for money or the organization as a whole. Giving should be a fun, joyful, and rewarding experience. If you can't cheerfully give money to an organization, you are better off to redirect those dollars to somewhere you feel better about or simply not give at all.

- **Give Deep, Not Wide** – Consider giving more money to fewer organizations than less money to a larger number of organizations. When you focus on a few select nonprofits, your giving becomes much more impactful to the organizations that you support. You also reduce the total amount of fundraising expenses that the organization spends in time and money following up with you.

It may take you a while to find nonprofit organizations that meet these criteria in your life. You may not be sure where your passion lies, or maybe you just haven't found the right organization to give to yet. Don't let this stop you from giving altogether. Until you have identified the three to five organizations that you want to support well, focus on the one or two that you already know that you want to give to. Over time, you will identify additional organizations that you want to support financially.

Consider Using a Donor-Advised Fund

Most people will write a check or make gifts online to the charities they support. If you give away a sizable amount of money each year (more than $25,000), you might consider giving through a donor-advised fund (DAF). A donor-advised fund allows you to set aside money in an investment account, receive an immediate tax deduction and give that money away at any point in the future. While using a donor-advised fund adds an extra step to the process of giving, there are some neat features that make using a donor-advised fund very useful:

- **One Giving Receipt** – Because you are effectively giving money to a charity that will later give away money to another charity, you receive a single tax receipt at the end of the year for all of the different nonprofits that you give money to. You no longer have to chase down small charities that don't have their books together to get a giving receipt to claim your gift on your taxes.

- **Giving Appreciated Assets** – If you have stocks, bonds, mutual funds or other securities that have appreciated in value, you can give those assets to your donor-advised fund without having to pay capital gains taxes on that money. For example, let's say that you have $10,000 in cash that you want to put in your donor-advised fund and $10,000 worth of a stock that has appreciated in value. Instead of putting the $10,000 into your donor-advised fund directly, you transfer the stock into the donor-advised fund, then re-buy the $10,000 position you had in that stock. While the end giving result is the same, you've eliminated the capital gains tax liability by giving the stock to your donor-advised fund and re-purchasing it with cash.

- **Flexible Giving** – With a donor-advised fund, you have the flexibility of distributing your money over time. If you want to receive a deduction for a charitable gift you make in one year and distribute the money the following year, you are free to do that.

- **Saving for a Big Gift** – You might want to save up over time for a very large gift, say $100,000 or $1,000,000, so that you can fund a large project or fund a new organization. With a donor-advised fund, you can set money aside over time and invest the money into mutual funds. Any interest or capital gains earned by the investments while in your donor-advised fund will be tax free. You will also receive current tax deductions for the deposits you make while saving up over a period of years for your big gift. When you've reached your desired dollar amount, you can sell the investment inside of your donor-advised fund and have a check issued to the charity of your choice.

- **Anonymous Giving** – If you want to make an anonymous gift to a nonprofit and write a check, it will never be truly anonymous because someone had to cash your check or process your credit card to receive the gift. Even when you want your giving to be private, your name may still appear on an internal donor list and be widely known within the organization you are giving to. With a donor-advised fund, you can make a truly anonymous gift. The organization administering the fund, such as Vanguard Charitable or Fidelity Charitable, can send a check to the nonprofit of your choice that doesn't have your name or the name of your donor-advised fund on it, so that your gifts are truly anonymous.

Donor-advised funds have some very useful features for serious givers, but they often have high minimums and per-gift minimums. Fidelity, Schwab, and T. Rowe Price all offer donor-advised funds. The minimum opening account balance ranges from $5,000 to $25,000. The minimum size for each gift made from the donor-advised fund ranges from $50 to $500. The brokerage managing your donor-advised fund will take a 0.5-0.6% management fee per year for any investments inside your account to cover their costs. I personally use the donor-advised fund offered by Vanguard Charitable, primarily because my other assets are at Vanguard and it's easy to transfer an appreciated stock from Vanguard to Vanguard Charitable.

A Note for Christians About Giving

Making charitable giving part of our everyday lives is especially important to those of us who are Christians. The Bible is clear that followers of God are to be generous givers. As early as the book of Genesis, Abel made an offering back to God from his flocks. Later in the Old Testament, the law prescribed that the Jewish people give a tithe (tenth) of their income to provide for the priests (the Levites), for the various festivals of their religion and for the poor. In the New Testament, Jesus states that those who follow him will be givers (Matthew 6:1-4). The early church set an example for future generations with their generosity (Acts 4:32-37), and the apostles instructed their followers to give generously and cheerfully to the church and to those in need (2 Corinthians 9:6-15). Let there be no doubt that generosity is a core tenet of the Christian faith.

Christians are called to use their financial resources to provide for three different categories of need. First, Christians are to feed the hungry, give drink to the thirsty, clothe the naked, care for the sick, and visit the imprisoned (Matthew 25:34-40). This call is echoed in the book of Proverbs, which says "whoever is kind to the poor lends to the Lord, and he will reward them for what they have done" (Proverbs 19:17). Second, Christians are called to support pastors and evangelists in their work. This calling is most clear in 1 Corinthians 9, where the Apostle Paul wrote that "those who preach the gospel should receive their living from the gospel." Every Christian should support their church financially at some level. Finally, Christians should help provide for the needs of other believers (Acts 4:32-37). When you become aware of a fellow Christian in financial need, you should follow the example of the early church and do whatever you can to help meet their needs.

Christians debate back and forth how much they should give to the church and to other charitable organizations. Some argue that Christians are supposed to give 10% of their income to the local church. Others agree with the concept of a tithe but believe that the money can be given to other religious organizations in addition to the local church. Still others say the tithe was only for the Jews and does not apply to Christians today because Christians are not under the Old Testament law. Theologians who are much smarter than I am have developed a variety of competing viewpoints on this issue, so I won't try to tell you definitively whether or not the tithe is still the standard for Christian giving. Rather, I will point you to Paul's words on giving and allow you to make your own decision about how much you should give:

> *Remember this: Whoever sows sparingly will also reap sparingly, and whoever sows generously will also reap generously. Each of you should give what you have decided in your heart to give, not reluctantly or under compulsion, for God loves a cheerful giver. And God is able to bless you abundantly, so that in all things at all times, having all that you need, you will abound in every good work. (2 Corinthians 9:6-8)*

Regardless of how much you give, Jesus is clear that Christians should be giving for the right reasons. He warned his disciples not to give for the sake of being admired by other people. He said: "Be careful not to practice your righteousness in front of others to be seen by them. If you do, you will have no reward from your Father in heaven" (Matthew 6:1). He further instructed his followers to give anonymously, saying that "when you give to the needy, do not let your left hand know what your right hand is doing, so that your giving may be in secret" (Matthew 6:3-4a).

Conclusion

While charitable giving might only seem tangentially related to wealth building, it has been an important part of my ten-year turnaround. I believe that those of us who are on the path to financial success have a responsibility to help others and do our part to address the world's problems with both our time and our money. If you are not currently giving to charity, I strongly encourage you to find a single organization whose mission you are passionate about and make your first gift. I believe that you will find charitable giving incredibly rewarding and more satisfying than owning more stocks, bonds or mutual fund shares. If you are already giving, I encourage you to consider how you can give more or give more effectively to the charitable causes that you care about.

My Charitable Giving Plan

What changes do you need to make in your life related to charitable giving? Do you need to start giving to charity? Do you need to commit to setting aside a fixed percentage of your income to charity each month? Do you need to identify a nonprofit that you can give both your time and money to? Do you need to start giving more to your church? Do you need to be more strategic about your current giving?

Write down what changes you are going to make in light of reading this chapter:

_____

_____

_____

_____

_____

_____

_____

_____

_____

_____

_____

_____

Action Steps

- ☐ Decide what percentage of your income you want to give to charity over the long term.

- ☐ Begin to identify three to five nonprofit organizations that you want to become a long-term supporter of with your time and money.

- ☐ Consider using a donor-advised fund for your giving.

Chapter Ten:
Putting it All Together

We have covered a lot of ground in *The Ten-Year Turnaround*. We have established long-term goals so that we know what financial freedom might look like. We have learned how to create more economic value in the marketplace and increase our income over time. We have discussed how lifelong learning and the power of personal networking can have an outsized impact on our income. We have covered basic financial and debt management skills. We have shown how to get better investment returns than the vast majority of individual investors receive. We have explored how to create an investment portfolio that will generate a lifetime income stream to provide for our needs. We have examined how to reduce our tax burdens, avoid lawsuits and protect ourselves from major negative financial events with the right types of insurance. Finally, we have considered how to discover the joy of charitable giving and how to give effectively.

While there are many different areas of personal development, personal finance and investing that you will need to master to achieve financial freedom, don't think that you need to master all of these knowledge areas at once. Remember that your ten-year turnaround is a decade-long journey of hard work, learning and determination. The path that you are going to take to attain financial freedom won't be immediately clear to you. You won't have it all figured out on day one and your journey to financial freedom will look different from everyone else's.

When I decided I was sick of working at McDonald's and was done living a life of financial mediocrity, I had no idea that I would go on to found a series of Internet businesses as a means of building my wealth. While hindsight is 20-20, we have no idea what the future holds. Although you might not be able to see the path to financial freedom right now, it doesn't mean that the path isn't there. You just don't see it yet. Begin your journey of sound financial management, effective investing, personal networking, lifelong learning and career advancement, and the path toward true financial freedom will reveal itself to you over time.

As you begin your ten-year turnaround, remember that there will be many twists and turns on your journey toward financial freedom. You might find that you take two steps forward, one step back, then a giant leap forward followed by another two steps back. There will be big, exhilarating wins and disappointing setbacks along the way. If you're doing well, don't get complacent and slow down. If you're not doing well, don't get discouraged and give up. Whether you're experiencing success or doing poorly, keep your eye on the prize of financial freedom and keep taking steps that will get you closer to financial freedom each and every day.

You have a lot of work ahead of you, but remember that there's many tangible and, to an even greater extent, intangible rewards waiting for you. If you follow the recommendations outlined in *The Ten-Year Turnaround*, eventually you will achieve true financial freedom. You will have a portfolio of investments that pay for your living expenses, and you'll have the freedom to quit your job and live your dream lifestyle. Unprecedented opportunities for world travel will open up. In your consumer life, money will cease to be an obstacle. You'll be able to be extremely generous, and your time won't be constrained by the nine-to-five grind. You can truly live a life of your own design.

Today is the first day of your ten-year turnaround. Go out, work hard, learn more, create value, manage money well, invest wisely, give generously and achieve financial freedom. You can do it. I believe in you.

Appendix:
Books for Lifelong Learners

I believe that reading nonfiction books is a critical component in the process of lifelong learning. By regularly reading books that explain how to do things you didn't previously know how to do, you become a better person and are capable of creating more value in the marketplace.

I recommend that everyone read at least one nonfiction book per month, with a focus on books that teach personal development, personal finance, career improvement, investing, religion, leadership, personal networking, history and business.

You are more than welcome to read fiction books and nonfiction books that don't fit into the categories above, but make sure to read at least one book that fits into those categories every month. I have compiled a list of 25 books that I believe you should read while completing your ten-year turnaround. In no particular order:

Personal Finance and Investing Books

Rich Dad, Poor Dad by Robert Kiyosaki

The Total Money Makeover by Dave Ramsey

The Ultimate Dividend Playbook by Josh Peters

Get Rich with Dividends by Marc Lichtenfeld

The Legacy Journey by Dave Ramsey

The Warren Buffett Way by Robert Hagstrom

I Will Teach You to Be Rich by Ramit Sethi

Personal Development Books

How to Win Friends and Influence People by Dale Carnegie

Never Eat Alone: And Other Secrets to Success, One Relationship at a Time by Keith Ferrazzi and Tahl Raz

The Compound Effect by Darren Hardy

Essentialism: The Disciplined Pursuit of Less by Greg McKeown

Eat That Frog by Brian Tracy

How to Get Rich by Felix Dennis

Think and Grow Rich by Napoleon Hill

7 Habits of Highly Effective People by Stephen Covey

Business and Career Books

Business Brilliant by Lewis Schiff

The Millionaire Fastlane by MJ Demarco

Mastering the Rockefeller Habits by Verne Harnish

The Four-Hour Workweek by Tim Ferris

The Personal MBA: Master the Art of Business by Josh Kaufman

The E-Myth Revisited by Michael Gerber

Freakonomics by Stephen Dubner & Steven Levitt

Good to Great by Jim Collins

The Millionaire Next Door by Thomas Stanley

Getting to Yes: Negotiating Agreement Without Giving in by Roger Fisher and William Ury

Thank You

Thank you for purchasing *The Ten-Year Turnaround* and taking the time to read it. Reading a nonfiction book can take quite a bit of time. Thank you for choosing to spend some of your valuable time digging through all the info I have to offer.

If you would like to share your thanks for this book, the best thing you can do is tell a friend about *The Ten-Year Turnaround* or buy them a copy. You can also show your appreciation for this book by leaving a review where you bought it. To leave a review on Amazon, visit the Amazon product page at TenYearTurnaround.com. Please be honest with your review and with how this book has or has not helped you on your journey to achieve your long-term financial goals. I want everyone to know if and/or how this book has changed your life in any significant way.

You can follow me online at my personal blog, MattPaulson.com. You can also follow me on Twitter (@MatthewDP).

If we have met in real life, feel free to add me as a friend on Facebook (facebook.com/matthewpaulson). If we have not met in real life, you are still welcome to "follow" me on Facebook.

I am also on LinkedIn (linkedin.com/in/matthewpaulson) and AngelList (angel.co/matthewpaulson).

If you would like to hear me talk about various topics, feel free to check out the interviews I have done at mattpaulson.com/interviews.

Thank you and God Bless,

Matthew Paulson

May 2016

Acknowledgements

I would like to express my sincere gratitude to my many friends, family members, and business acquaintances that have encouraged me while I have pursued various entrepreneurial adventures over the last decade.

I would like to thank my wife, Karine, for being incredibly supportive, putting up with my unusual work schedule, and trusting me to provide for our family through my business.

I would like to thank my children, Micah and Adylin, for the many smiles they put on my face every day.

I would like to thank my business partners and team members, including David Anicetti, Donna Helling, Todd Kolb, Don Miller, Tyler Prins, Rebecca McKeever, Jason Shea, Stevie Shea and Toi Williams. Without them, my companies would not be where they are today.

Finally, I would like to express my gratitude to the many talented people who worked on this book.

I would like to thank Elisa Doucette and her team at Craft Your Content for editing this book and fixing my many grammar and spelling errors.

I would like to thank Rebecca McKeever for proofreading this book.

I would like to thank Ellen Jesperson for designing the cover of this book.

I would like to thank James Woosley for doing this book's layout.

I would like to thank Stu Gray and Toby Lyles for putting together the audio version of this book.

And I would like to thank Perrin Carrell for helping to promote this book.

About the Author

Matthew Paulson is a serial entrepreneur if there ever was one. His largest business, MarketBeat.com, publishes a financial newsletter to more than 400,000 investors on a daily basis. He is also a partner at GoGo Photo Contest, a company that helps animal welfare groups raise money through donate-to-vote photo contest fundraisers. Finally, he is a partner at USGolfTV, a digital publishing company that produces a regionally syndicated television show and other content for the golf industry.

Matthew holds a B.S. in Computer Science and an M.S. in Information Systems from Dakota State University. He also holds an M.A. in Christian Leadership from Sioux Falls Seminary.

Matthew's first book, *40 Rules for Internet Business Success*, shared the principles and strategies that he's used to build a seven-figure Internet business (and multiple six-figure businesses) from scratch. Matthew's second book, *Email Marketing Demystified*, provides a step-by-step guide for any entrepreneur to implement email marketing in their business. Matthew's third book, *The Ten-Year Turnaround*, teaches people to increase their income, build wealth and attain true financial freedom.

Matthew resides in Sioux Falls, South Dakota, where he lives with his wife, Karine, and his two children, Micah and Adylin.

Connect with Matthew at:

- Matthew's Personal Blog: MattPaulson.com
- AngelList: angel.co/matthewpaulson
- Facebook: facebook.com/matthewpaulson
- LinkedIn: LinkedIn.com/in/matthewpaulson
- Twitter: twitter.com/matthewdp
- Email: matt@mattpaulson.com